# Practical Ideas for Cutting Costs and Ways to Generate Alternative Revenue Sources

Tim L. Adsit
George Murdock

Rowman & Littlefield Education
Lanham, Maryland • Toronto • Oxford
2005

Published in the United States of America
by Rowman & Littlefield Education
A Division of Rowman & Littlefield Publishers, Inc.
A wholly owned subsidary of The Rowman & Littlefield Publishing Group,
Inc.
4501 Forbes Boulevard, Suite 200, Lanham, Maryland 20706
www.rowmaneducation.com

PO Box 317
Oxford
OX2 9RU, UK

British Library Cataloguing in Publication Information Available

**Library of Congress Cataloging-in-Publication Data**
Adsit, Tim L., 1948–
  Practical ideas for cutting costs and ways to generate alternative revenue
sources / Tim L. Adsit, George Murdock.
    p. cm.
  Includes bibliographical references and index.
  ISBN 1-57886-265-5 (pbk. : alk. paper)
  1. Education—United States—Finance. 2. Education—United States—Cost
control. 3. School management and organization—United States. I. Murdock,
George, 1942– II. Title.
  LB2825.A563 2005
  371.2'06—dc22
                                                              2005004181

∞™ The paper used in this publication meets the minimum requirements of
American National Standard for Information Sciences—Permanence of Paper
for Printed Library Materials, ANSI/NISO Z39.48-1992.
Manufactured in the United States of America.

# Contents

# Preface

At no time in the history of public education has there been such a dramatic discrepancy between accelerated standards and expectations and adequate funding for our schools. Much has been written about how to achieve new expectations in the realm of student achievement. Much has also been written about the need for accountability and the restructuring of how education dollars are spent. Unfortunately, most of the input regarding the need for "belt-tightening" is unaccompanied by any tangible solutions or suggestions and results only in hollow rhetoric or convenient political sound bytes.

Our journey into meaningful avenues for cost savings in public education is clearly an exception. It would be literally impossible for any school official to read this book and not find a number of viable possibilities for saving money. Previewers and colleagues have been quite fascinated with the book because it is timely and because anyone who buys the book will more than pay for it with direct savings. We have walked the same path as our colleagues; this book offers practical ideas that can be readily implemented. What's more, even though it provides several hundred pages of thoughtful ideas and suggestions, it can best be viewed as an introduction to a broader conversation that surely must follow. We suspect that each reader will be able to add to our list of cost savings, ways to increase revenues and case studies, and that a supplement or sequel will soon be in order.

# Introduction

In public education, the mission traditionally has been to provide high-quality, effective programs and services at a reasonable cost to taxpayers to continuously improve student learning and achievement. Now, however, we are experiencing a dramatic change that will probably affect education for years to come: there simply is not enough money to continue in a "business as usual" manner.

For example, Gallup and Phi Delta Kappa polls recently asked Americans their opinions on many issues related to education in public schools. When respondents were asked to identify the biggest problems that public schools in their communities must deal with, "lack of funding/financial support" topped the list for the third straight year in a row (Gallup Poll 2002).

In the past several years, school districts, education services districts, and community colleges have considered a variety of cost-saving measures, some of which are successfully in use today. Others, previously put aside, now are being dusted off and reexamined. Even changes in state laws and rules may need to be considered. While a given idea may seem unacceptable, all options should be considered with an open mind in any analysis. Certainly, this is no time to reinvent the wheel, and we all stand to gain from those of us in the field of education who have successful practical experience with cost saving and revenue generating ideas.

The economic times demand that we take a fresh look at the way we operate, look for better ways, and ask questions we have never had to ask.

1

Yet arriving at creative solutions may be hampered by all-too-familiar obstacles: seeing only what we want and expect to see, being too close to a problem, a belief that money solves everything, resistance to change, failure to think outside the box, unwillingness to change our paradigm, and, of course, the traditions held sacred in our districts. However, as Albert Einstein once remarked, "The significant problems we face today [in education] cannot be solved at the same level of thinking we were at when we created them in the first place." If we keep doing what we have always done, we will keep getting what we have always gotten. We don't have a lack of money problem in education as much as we have a lack of creative ideas.

Since 1976, when Tim Adsit served in his first superintendent position, he has been collecting and implementing thoughts and ideas on managing costs and generating alternative revenue sources from local educators around Oregon and the United States. These ideas are offered by educators for consideration as potential ways to creatively manage costs and generate revenues. The ideas are practical and time-tested, and they work. Some of the ideas may be helpful to you, others may not. Think of this book as you would a trip to the supermarket: Don't buy everything on the shelves all at once, take what you need at the time, and use it to fit your particular situation. Make this book a desk reference you consult daily and integrate the useful ideas that match your needs with your leadership style.

We hope that many of the suggestions will be useful in your school district and will stimulate administrators to identify many more creative ideas than those presented. Through experience, we have found that by reviewing these ideas with others, a synergistic effect will take place as you begin to reflect on the creative ideas presented and you will think of other creative ideas that fit your district's needs. We encourage you to write down these new ideas as they come to mind during group brainstorming sessions. A word of caution, however: Be careful to check the legality of an idea in your state. However, even if you find that you cannot implement some of the practical ideas presented because of an existing state or federal statute or regulation, don't give up; instead write your state department of education for a waiver or work to change the law. Many of the existing barriers and obstacles to effective school management were quietly pushed and lobbied into law by special-interest groups when taxpayer interests were not well organized. It is now time to seek reform. The public and its legislators across the nation are watching and listening and they expect more quality, productivity, accountability, change, and improvement. This book has been developed to provide school district administrators with the experience gained by others facing a decline in resources. Many of the suggestions offered in these pages bring about greater cost effectiveness and even improved productivity. The ideas are not all original, exhaustive, or comprehensive or wholly applicable to any one school system. The review of the literature and bibliography are not exhaustive or up to the minute. But the ideas presented are time-tested and proven to work. The chapters have been organized by what seems to these writers to be a logical progression, for the sake of economy, and so that each chapter and the appendices materials included can be directed to appropriate district personnel, board members, advisory groups, or community focus groups.

Chapter 1 briefly reviews the literature on managing decline in resources and discusses the problem of declining funds for schools and solution strategies.

Chapter 2 lists cost-saving tips for district and school-level administration.

Chapter 3 lists cost-saving tips in curriculum, instruction, vocational education, special education, student services, and media services.

Chapter 4 presents cost-saving tips for support services: building and grounds, maintenance, pupil transportation, and food services.

Chapter 5 addresses cost savings for community colleges.

Chapter 6 briefly reviews the literature on generating alternative revenue sources in education and provides a sample of strategic plans and creative ideas for generating alternative revenues used in many districts today.

Some expanded cost-saving ideas are described further at the end of each chapter. If a suggestion seems appropriate to more than one area, it is presented more than once. Several case studies have also been included at the end of appropriate chapters.

Furthermore, there are approaches to cutting costs that seem to apply to almost any program area. For example:

- Have you considered the skills of your staff outside the areas of their professional training? You may have access to good part-time carpenters, mechanics, and so forth, or those who could help with drama, music, athletics, and similar activities because of hobbies or other work experience.
- Have you considered exchange/trade-off arrangements with local business or industry (e.g., free lunches for volunteers to work with disabled children, or businesses to provide on-site learning settings, work experience stations, or consultants in exchange for use of school facilities for their employees in the evenings)?
- Have you considered different avenues of cooperative interagency agreements between schools, between districts, through ESDs, cities, counties, or community colleges, or cooperatives for sharing resources (e.g., mechanics, repair and maintenance contracts, or for group purchase of materials, supplies, or commodities)?
- Are you utilizing vocational education classes for construction projects such as bookcases, partitions, rebuilding, or refinishing furniture?
- Have you fully explored all angles of parent/volunteer involvement such as garage sales, auctions, flea markets, donations, help as playground supervisors, or help locating used furniture or equipment from business or government offices where they are cutting back or upgrading their existing inventory?

You'll find these ideas and more in the following chapters.

# 1

# The Problem of Declining Funds for Schools

This is a time of economic crisis for Oregon public schools and schools across the nation. While in recent years school districts have found ways to adjust to the passage of statewide tax limitations, limited federal and state support, as well as voter unwillingness to approve tax increases, there are indications that more adjustments will be needed before matters get better. For example, the state of Oregon is experiencing a $994 million shortfall in projected revenues for the current 2001–2003 biennium and $1 billion shortfalls are projected for each of the next two bienniums in the 2003–2005 and 2005–2007 years, barring the establishment of any new sources of revenues (Oregon Legislative Revenue Office 2002).

The purposes of chapter 1 are to survey current economic, social, and political factors that may affect public school resources, and to suggest approaches that districts can take in an effort to maintain educational quality with fewer resources.

## WHAT WE KNOW

A gap has been developing between rising educational costs and taxpayers' willingness and ability to pay; recent property tax limitations, school levy defeats, and national surveys bear this trend out. Coupled with the state's economic picture, shortfalls in anticipated revenues as well as legislator reluctance to identify, come to consensus on, and legally establish new sources of revenues and the passage of new state and federal mandates designed to increase accountability and improve education (e.g., the No Child Left Behind Act), the challenge to maintain educational quality becomes even greater. Here are some of the facts:

- Education is one of the biggest businesses in the United States. Total expenditures for public elementary and secondary education alone are approaching $336 billion for the 2000–2001 fiscal year (National Center for Educational Statistics 2000).
- Projected public education revenues for the 2000–2001 fiscal year are approximately $354 billion (National Center for Education Statistics 2000).
- State, local, and private expenditures accounted for over 90 percent of spending, with the federal government contributing about 10 percent to support students of all ages (U.S. Department of Education 1997).
- Nationally, total per pupil expenditures have risen from $5,520 in 1994–1995 (National Center for Education Statistics 1999) to an estimated $6,585 in the 1999–2000 academic year (National Center for Education Statistics 2000).
- In the state of Oregon, for example, we have less money today than in the 1990–1991 fiscal year, because inflation and student growth have outdistanced the state school fund appropriations and because the student growth has been greater in high-cost special education and English-language learner groups (Heiligman 2002).
- Nationally, schools are spending an increasing proportion of their instructional budgets on special education, although estimates differ by district and state (Protheroe 1997; Johnston 1998; Parrish 2000).
- State school fund revenues in Oregon, for example, have increased, but real revenues per student have declined because of inflation and increases in student enrollment (Heiligman 2002).
- Nationally, per pupil expenditures are expected to increase to $9,204 in 2009–2010 (National Center for Education Statistics 1999).
- In Oregon, for example, some school districts' cost increases were above inflation. Major cost drivers include health care cost increases, declining enrollment, and changes in student demographics (Heiligman 2002).

• Education has truly become the largest single spending category in all the states (National Conference of State Legislatures 1996).

## WHAT WE BELIEVE

In addition to the foregoing factual indicators, there is other evidence pointing to increasing difficulties in maintaining current resource levels. Concerns about equitable and adequate distribution of educational opportunities are matched by equally pressing worries and perceptions about productivity and efficiency in public schooling. Although historically the productivity problem has been about rising resources with flat or only slightly rising student achievement, the future challenge will be to produce substantially higher student achievement with flat or stable resources (Odden and Clune 1995). National experts have managed to reach agreement on three points: Available resources are shrinking even in good economic times (prior to the recent recession that began officially in the spring of 2001); research should uncover how funds are actually being spent; and schools will have to discover more cost-effective ways to use existing resources (Hadderman 1998).

The public's perception of school effectiveness is often based on fragmentary and sometimes inaccurate evidence. People often make judgments about public schools on the basis of little evidence, seeking reinforcement of their current perceptions of schools. Too, media coverage has in many ways reinforced the ideas that schools are failing. One indication of such media influence can be seen in recent Gallup polls where a very high percent rated schools in their own community "A" or "B," but a much lower percent rated schools this well nationally. Similarly, those with children in public school gave higher grades than those without. In both cases, it is likely that local sources of information offset press criticism at the national level (Gallup 2001).

In general the public has incomplete knowledge of school budgets and the school budgeting process. Low turnout at district budget hearings and board meetings, along with little budget coverage in the media, would suggest that school patrons generally are uninformed about the costs of the programs that they are buying. This knowledge vacuum may then be filled with negativity, hearsay, and supposition. When, for example, additional resources are "found" after a levy defeat, the district's credibility is undermined and more speculation results. Thus, there is little reason to discourage broad citizen participation in the budgeting process.

Taxpayers feel that they have little control over the economic factors that directly affect their well-being (e.g., inflation, job security, interest rates, and taxes). Voting against tax increases is one of the few ways in which taxpayers can express those feelings.

As long as present trends continue, the proportion of federal and local support for education will diminish and public schools will depend to a greater extent on state revenues, which are currently experiencing unanticipated shortfalls due to the economy, at least in Oregon. This trend is likely to continue, as equalization efforts shift more financial responsibility for schools to the state level (Protheroe 1997).

In the face of rising costs for education, taxpayers are more likely to demand evidence that educational quality is also increasing. With per pupil costs rising at a faster rate than the costs of other products and services, taxpayers want to know if they are getting what they are paying for. As productivity becomes more of an issue, the public is asking for either curtailment of school resources or more performance-based accountability and evidence of productivity improvement on the part of schools. For example, consider the state and national assessment tests currently being implemented in all states across the nation and the new GASB 34 regulations (Government Accounting Standards Board, Statement 34). The result could be a narrowing of the schools' mission with a greater focus to economize on the costs of education.

Researchers are divided on the productivity issue in public education, which is a debate over whether money matters in education outcomes. Researchers such as Eric Hanushek (1996) found little advancement in student achievement over the years that can be traced to increased funding. Others, on the other hand, are more optimistic, claiming that some expenditures are tied to improved student achievement (Hedges, Laine, and Greenwald 1994; Kazal-Thresher 1993).

For example, in Oregon, after a decade of targeted spending on school improvement efforts, public schools have made some fairly impressive gains in reading and math scores. Oregon's public schools have changed after a decade of targeted school improvement—in spite of the fact that Oregon's schools had less money per student on an inflation-adjusted basis; we still saw improvements for students in achievement gains.

Increasing costs, declining public confidence in school effectiveness, the local and statewide effects of an economic recession, and projected shortfalls in state revenues for school fund support pose an unprecedented challenge for schools in maintaining quality programs and services. Some overall issues in strategic planning during periods of declining resources are discussed below, along with a brief review of the literature on managing decline.

## A BRIEF REVIEW OF THE LITERATURE ON MANAGING DECLINE

The literature on the management of declining resources is replete with definitions of terms such as *conflict*, which means to show antagonism or irreconcilability; competitive or opposing action of incompatibles; an antagonistic state or action; or a breakdown in the standard mechanism of decision making.

The concept *decremental* means a gradual decrease in quantity or quality — for example, budget cutting across the board in approximately equal reductions to all departments, extending replacement cycles, implementing hiring freezes, reducing force through employee attrition, freezing expenditure accounts, and rationing necessary operational supplies.

*Theories of decline* concentrate on "natural selection," which focuses on the population level, and "organizational decline," which focuses on the organizational level.

*Causes of decline* include several topologies. Decline is based on four types of changes in the external environment (Zammuto and Cameron 1982): (1) erosion: a continuous decline in an organization's size; (2) contraction: a sudden and unexpected removal of resources or drop in demand for the organization's products or services; (3) dissolution: a gradual shift from one niche to another; and (4) collapse: a rapid and unanticipated change in the market. Likewise, these types of changes can be brought about by three constraints imposed by the external environment: physical, biological, and social.

*Responses to decline* show that a successful strategic management response to decline requires the following four conditions be addressed: (1) a multiyear time frame for implementation; (2) a significant reallocation and reconfiguration of the organization's resources; (3) substantial changes in the organization's structure and work force; and (4) that the organization's problems, mission, and possible alternatives of action must be comprehensively evaluated and the results acted upon (Levine 1978). Further, Levine identified potential organizational consequences of decremental strategies as being human resource erosion, overcentralization, allocation shifts, and decisional paralysis (Levine 1978).

Factors affecting the *selection of a strategic management approach* are many. For example, the effectiveness of the management plan depends on the "contingency relationships" between the management strategy and the situation; the use of strategic planning requires that the organization have the internal capacity to monitor and predict its cost and to provide specific programs and services; strategic management requires the examination of alternative delivery options; and fiscal stress will close some windows of organizational opportunity but will open others.

*Responding to organizational decline* may take on three categories of response: avoidance, defense, or learning (Bourgeois 1985). Four categories of managerial behavior identified by Miles and Snow include domain defenders, reluctant reactors, anxious analyzers, and enthusiastic prospectors (Miles and Snow 1978). And four categories of managerial responses include generating, reacting, defending, and preventing (Whetton 1980).

*Organizational functions* necessary to effectively manage the decline process include an effective forecasting and planning capacity, clearly understood levels of decision-making authority, a viable management philosophy and process to help employees define the organization's future, a process for rapid and accurate feedback between affected parties, budgetary flexibility to maximize the use of scarce organizational resources, performance incentives for employees, the ability to identify the core services of the organization, the ability to target available resources to high-priority programs and cuts to low-priority programs, and the ability to successfully link service and program expenditures to the organization's decision-making process (Levine 1985).

*Tasks leaders must attend to* during decline include managing awareness, alternatives, involvement, fair play, support, disclosure, understanding, and blame (Hardy 1987). Likewise, Sutton found that tasks leaders must attend to during times of decline in resources include disbanding, sustaining, shielding, informing, blaming, delegating, inventing, and coping (Sutton 1983).

*General assumptions and conclusions* with regard to managing decline are that leaders must view the organization's environment clearly, interpret the environment correctly, develop strategies about how one should respond, develop, and implement programs to effectively reposition the organization within its altered environment, and implement the organizational adaptations necessary to adjust to the conditions that brought about the decline (McKelvey 1988).

A review of the literature on *crisis management* in organizations identifies basic dimensions of a crisis as being a turning point in an unfolding sequence of events and actions, a situation in which the requirement for action is high in the minds of the organization's participants, or a threat to the goals and objectives of those involved; followed by an important organization outcome whose consequences and effects will shape the future of the parties involved, a convergence of events whose combination produces a new set of organizational realities and circumstances, a period in which uncertainties about the assessment of the situation and the alternatives for dealing with it will increase, a period of time or a situation in which control over events and their effects decreases; characterized by a sense of urgency, which often produces stress and anxiety among the organization's participants or a circumstance (or set of circumstances) in which information available to participants is usually inadequate; also characterized by increased time pressures on those involved; marked by changes in the relations among the organization's members; and a time of increased tensions among the organization's members (Wiener and Kahn 1962).

Likewise, *basic characteristics of a crisis* are that it represents an acute rather than chronic challenge, though the length of the crisis is usually unspecified; produces changes in employee behavior that are frequently pathological; is characterized by threat to the goals of the person or organization involved; is relative in that what is perceived to be a crisis for one participant may not be for another; and produces tensions in individuals, including physical stress and mental anxiety (Miller and Iscoe 1963).

*Conceptual components* of crisis include threat (a potential hindrance to some state or goal desired by the organizational unit) and time (decision time is typically short). When the crisis arises, existing situations must be altered. Conceptual components also include surprise; there is a lack of awareness by the decision makers and participants that the crisis situation is likely to occur (Herman 1972).

*Management style preference* of leaders was studied by Smart. He used Douglas McGregor's Theory X and Theory Y characteristics of leadership and found that the task-oriented Theory X leader believed that work is inherently distasteful to most people; most people are not ambitious, have little desire for responsibility, and prefer to be directed; most people have little capacity for creativity in solving organizational problems; motivation occurs only at the physiological and safety levels; and most people must be closely controlled and often coerced to achieve organizational objectives. On the other hand, Smart found that the process-oriented Theory Y leader believed that work is as natural as play, if the conditions are favorable; self-control is often indispensable in achieving organizational goals; the capacity for creativity in solving organizational problems is widely distributed in the population; motivation occurs at the social, esteem, and self-actualization levels, as well as at the physiological and security levels; and people can be self-directed and creative at work if properly motivated (Smart 1980).

*Power and influence* during crisis was studied by French and Raven in their 1959 study and they identified the following types of power: (1) expert power, where subordinates assume the leader's judgment is correct because of the leader's special competency; (2) referent power, which is based upon the feelings of the subordinate toward the leader as a person; (3) legitimate power or legal authority, which is based upon the subordinate's belief that compliance must occur because of the leader's formal position over the subordinate; (4) reward power, which exists when subordinates comply in the hope of getting something of value in return from the leader; and (5) coercive power, which occurs when subordinates follow the leader's directives to avoid potential punishment should they fail to comply (French and Raven 1959).

Likewise, Raven and Kruglanski identified information power, which is the influence generated from the possession and/or control of information not held by others in the organization (Raven and Kruglanski 1975) and Hersey and Goldsmith identified connection power, which is commonly referred to as networking power (i.e., the ability to make access into, use, and/or coordinate resources from one or more networks (Hersey and Goldsmith 1979).

*Conflict management* has been studied by many researchers. Blake and Moulton identified behaviors exhibited when confronted with conflict as being suppressing, confronting, compromising, avoiding, and soothing (Blake and Moulton 1964); Thomas identified and added cooperating and asserting behaviors (Thomas 1976).

In addition, *models used in addressing and managing conflict* include competing (attempting to satisfy one's own concerns at the expense of the other party's concerns), accommodating (satisfying the other party's concerns at the neglect of one's own), avoiding (neglecting both one's own and the other party's concerns by sidestepping or postponing the raising of conflict producing issues), collaborating (attempting to satisfy the concerns of both parties through problem solving focused on finding a mutually agreeable solution), and compromising (seeking a middle-ground position requiring give and take from both parties) (Thomas 1976).

*Predicators of a manager's success in dealing with conflict* include possessing a high level of intelligence; a personality characterized by dominance, self-confidence, and manipulative sociability; a lifelong pattern of successful endeavors; a better education than the average person, demonstrating greater conscientiousness in school; an openness and experiencing a less restrictive upbringing in his or her family situation; and a search for achievement, autonomy, and recognition more than seeking money or interesting work (Dunnette 1964).

Likewise, *common characteristics shared by effective crisis managers* include being able to adopt and support a team management philosophy, being a strong team player, possessing the ability to delegate, being a strong communicator, possessing a high degree of salesmanship talent, being a strong decision maker, possessing excellent judgment, and being an expert in time management.

Finally, with respect to a summary, conclusions, and recommendations, in a study entitled "Managing Decline: A Study to Identify the Leadership Strategies and Skills Used by Oregon Public School Superintendents to Manage Organizational Decline," Dodds summarized past practices and found that with respect to organizational goals, school boards experiencing organizational decline as a result of reductions in the organization's level of fiscal resources essentially adopt the primary organizational goals imposed by state law. To achieve the organizational goal of reduction, school boards have generally adopted four criteria to guide their district's actions: protect the district's instructional program at all costs; protect the extracurricular programs if possible; make the large reductions in the areas of building maintenance, food service, and transportation; and become as efficient as possible in providing the programs and services that remain in the district's operating budget (Dodds 1990). In contrast to what has been recommended in the literature, Dodds found districts have not further centralized the organization's decision-making process during decline. He also found that during decline, administrators seek information to guide their decision from a very narrow spectrum of potential sources, and districts almost exclusively adopt short-term organizational strategies to manage the decline process (Dodds 1990).

However, not all school boards experiencing organizational decline as a result of reductions in the organization's level of fiscal resources adopt the primary organizational goals imposed by state law. For example, the foundations of decision making, particularly in many smaller, rural school districts across America, where in most cases the path to cost cutting is fairly straightforward, are, unfortunately, rarely followed since the foundation for decision making in such an environment is generally emotional rather than economically rational. It may be cost effective to contract for transportation, food service, and maintenance/custodial services, but in areas where decent jobs are sparse and the current drivers, food service workers, and janitors have lived in the community for years and are related to half the town, the topic just doesn't get addressed. The economics of rural America are so shaky in many areas these days that school jobs are precious and therefore are being preserved even in the wake of necessary cuts. Refer, for example, to the publication available from Northwest Regional Educational Laboratory entitled "Distress and Survival: Rural Schools, Education, and the Importance of Community" (Miller 1991).

Likewise, Monk and Haller (1986) conducted detailed case studies of small, rural towns and their schools in New York State and they describe the dilemma facing rural school districts and communities:

> In some respects the image Americans have of their small towns—shaded, tree-lined streets; a solid sense of community identity; friendly, caring neighbors; a reasonably stable economic base oriented to the surrounding farms; and a shared set . . . of values—describes the villages we visited. . . . In every locality, the economy presented problems. The root of these problems was perceived to be the gradual drain of business and industry out of

the community . . . whatever the cause, it was clear that each village was in some economic difficulty. This difficulty manifested itself in numerous ways. Perhaps the most obvious was a generally high rate of unemployment. . . . The state of the local economies also had less obvious consequences . . . a drain of youth out of these villages to areas that offer greater economic opportunity . . . the lack of leisure activities for youth . . . people drive, sometimes lengthy distances, to work in neighboring small cities. (Monk and Haller 1986, 25–28)

Probably the most significant theme to emerge from Monk and Haller's case studies (1986) was the central role the school played in the community. In these economically declining communities, the school remained one of the only, if not the only, viable institution. It served as a gathering place, a key recreational facility, an employer, and maybe most importantly, "a stable pattern in the web of social life that binds individuals together. It is what makes a community something more than an aggregation of people" (Monk and Haller 1986, 28). This sense of community in rural America's schools and towns makes decision making in such an economically declining environment emotional rather than economically rational.

In addition, Dodds found superintendents' perceptions of important skills needed during decline include communication, ability to manage multiple problems, engaging in effective human relations, effectively managing the organization's fiscal resources, effective problem solving, and effectively managing the rising levels of organizational conflict (Dodds 1990). Further, a summary of superintendents' and board members' perceptions showed that superintendents reported experiencing an increased level of personal stress and they felt lonely; generally, younger superintendents expressed a concern that their experience in leading a declining organization may have damaged their professional reputations as effective organizational leaders; superintendents and school boards reported receiving essentially no assistance from anyone to help them understand the decline process or to provide guidance in managing the decline process (a good reason for this book to be published); and superintendents reported a reluctance to share their personal frustrations and problems with fellow colleagues. As a result, they avoided such discussions and kept their frustrations to themselves (Dodds 1990).

And, recommendations in the literature reviewed include assessing the severity of the situation, seeking outside assistance in planning for retrenchment, and seeking input from others before important organizational decisions are made; being equally attentive to managing issues of organizational risk and human relations; taking the time to reevaluate what the district's goals are to be during decline and use those goals to anchor the district's decision-making process; superintendents should use alternative and multiple forms of power to lead their declining organizations; and acknowledging that organizational conflict will exist and attempt to resolve it (Dodds 1990).

## Analyzing the Situation

The first order of business in budget planning is to determine the extent of the problem in meeting district resource needs. Historically, at least in Oregon, prior to the passage of tax limitation measures, a school district and its local community, in effect, "negotiated" an acceptable rate of revenue increase based on several years' experience with local school levy measures. However, today, after the passage of tax limitations that effectively eliminated local control, when such factors as unemployment, local economic growth, and community conflict over education change drastically, a district may find that the traditional level of voter support has also changed. One's ability to negotiate and communicate with one's local constituency is still important, but not as important as one's ability to negotiate and communicate with state legislators. Adequate planning and a realistic analysis of the situation, however, will help to ensure that school boards and administrators have a range of alternatives available as they select solution strategies for dealing with declining revenues.

In analyzing its present and projected fiscal situation, a district may find it useful to describe the anticipated balance between income and budget needs. Each district is unique and will face altogether different planning strategies and agendas. For example, one district may expect to maintain a balance between income and expenditures needed to sustain current programs. Another district, on the other hand, may foresee a short-term deficit necessitating immediate expenditure cuts, but a return to current revenue levels over the long term adjusted for inflation. And yet another district might project the need to make budget cuts immediately, which are not likely to be restored within the next four to five years due to projected state revenue shortfalls. A shortfall is the percentage discrepancy between resources actually received or anticipated and resources needed to maintain current programs and services and a balanced budget. Each of these fiscal projections has distinct implications for the way in which the budget is adjusted and how each district analyzes cost-cutting alternatives.

A large number of variables determine a district's budget, many of which cannot be predicted with any degree of certainty. Most variables

**Table 1.1. Variables with Fiscal Impact**

| Revenue | Expenditures | External | Internal | Variable |
|---|---|---|---|---|
| x | | | x | student growth/loss |
| x | | | x | state funding (gain/loss) |
| x | | | x | new initiatives/legislation |
| x | | | x | equity or other lawsuits |
| x | | | x | property assessed values |
| x | | | x | fiscal relief cycle |
| | x | | x | ESD service resolutions |
| | x | | x | public employee retirement system % pickup |
| | x | | x | retirements |
| | x | | x | resignations |
| | x | | x | tax anticipation notes interest rates |
| | x | | x | adhering to mandates |
| | x | | x | inflation impact |
| | x | | x | bond issue |
| x | x | | x | length of fiscal downturn |
| x | x | | x | student fees |
| x | x | | x | cash reserve levels |
| | x | | x | "privatization of services," e.g., transportation, food custodial, etc. |
| | x | | x | reduction in force |
| | x | | x | length of school year, number of student days per week |
| | x | | x | school closures |
| | x | | x | program decisions, academic and extracurricular, whether to retain, reduce, or eliminate |
| | x | | x | negotiations, salaries, and benefits |

relate to either revenues or expenditures and are controlled either externally or internally. The value of the matrix in Table 1.1 is that the district can clearly identify the variables that it controls by its decision making. Most external variables will cycle, regardless of what the budget committee or board decides. Any "internal" variables can be included in the local decision-making process.

Knowledge or at least estimates of the following will also help clarify the financial picture beyond the immediate future:

- Future student enrollment by grade.
- Demographic, economic, and political trends at the local and state levels affecting voter willingness to approve tax increases, requests for salary increases, nonpersonnel costs, and attitudes toward school closure, and school choice or homeschool initiatives.
- General economic and political trends at the state level affecting state school fund support, property tax relief, grant-in-aid programs, timber revenues, property tax limitation initiatives and measures, and so forth.
- Trends in the level and method of federal support for education.
- Budgets and audit reports tracking district resources and expenditures over time.

While future costs and income cannot be pinpointed on the basis of such factors and variables, a range of "best" to "worst" estimates will make contingency planning possible.

## Budget Development Considerations

Since no two school districts are alike, there are few solutions to budget problems that apply equally across all districts, but there are a number of cost-cutting measures from which to choose. These need to be analyzed and weighed carefully before they can be translated into an operating budget. This process of resolving budget concerns may occur in five suggested stages: setting ground rules, parameters, and policies; involving staff and community; examining cost-cutting alternatives; presenting options to the board of directors; and evaluating the impact of budget reduction.

## Setting Ground Rules, Parameters, and Policies

Clear budget-reduction policies need to be established in advance, specifying the responsibilities of the school board, budget committee, superintendent, central administrative staff, building principals, teachers, building or district site councils or executive councils, and citizen advisory committees. Each group's involvement should be understood in advance. Other policies to establish might include:

- The board's overall educational goals and priorities;
- The preferred mix of instruction, support, and administrative functions;
- Policies on class size;
- Support for special student populations such as talented and gifted, handicapped and non-English-speaking students, and recognizing the need for meeting maintenance of effort requirements in special education;
- Priorities regarding extracurricular activities;
- Provisions for student transportation;
- Support for continuing staff development; and
- Goals for curriculum improvement.

Communication on such matters helps set the stage for coherent long-range planning.

## Involving Staff and Community

Staff and community expect, and sometimes demand, to know how and why some budget decisions are made, and they want to be involved in making the decisions. Involvement of both groups is likely to bring the following advantages:

- Increased awareness and understanding of school matters—an informed staff and community will help the district make sound decisions.
- Increased support—people support decisions more when they help make them.

- Enhanced student achievement and attitudes toward school—students tend to achieve more and place a higher value on learning when parents get involved in school.
- Improved staff morale—when the community gets involved in schools, it is likely that staff morale will improve.
- Greater creativity in solving budget problems—school administrators' blind spots and paradigms may be overcome when staff members and citizens take part.

With open lines of communication and broad-based input, administrators can help to ease tensions that may arise when difficult decisions have to be made. When working with district staff:

- The superintendent should meet with union leadership as soon as practicable to explain the financial crisis. Suggest that they look at negotiated contracts to see if some changes could help reduce costs. Reassure the unions that no unilateral action is contemplated.
- Set forth any legal, contractual, state, or federal standards compliance limitations, such as maintenance of effort regulations, which may affect budgeting. Make clear the extent to which these factors can or cannot be negotiated or "waived."
- Inform and involve all segments of the staff—building-level administrators, professional staff, support and maintenance staff, and bus drivers. *Establish study groups using the ideas, coding system, prioritization processes, and group input materials found in this book to analyze suggestions, set priorities among those suggestions, draft impact statements, and make recommendations.*

*Involve the Community*

Establish study groups in the community or utilize existing ones (e.g., local school/PTA committees, special task forces, district advisory councils, booster clubs) to analyze ideas and make recommendations; provide them with all available data; and ask staff members to serve as resource personnel, giving their views on the probable impact of various proposals made by the groups. Once again, use the ideas, coding system, prioritization processes, and group input materials found in this book to analyze suggestions, set priorities among those suggestions, draft impact statements, and make recommendations.

- Survey the community regarding educational priorities and utilize the results when making decisions.
- Organize local school or district site councils to serve as liaison among community, school-level administrative, and school board interests.
- Install a district telephone "hotline" number, website, or e-mail address that citizens can call or contact for answers to their questions. The hotline, website, or e-mail address should be open on a daily basis, and the personnel who answer inquiries should be fully informed of the most recent budget and policy decisions.
- Keep the public informed through the media, meetings, and district newsletters; provide two-way communication as much as possible.
- Explain fully the reasons for increases in budget costs that exceed what might be expected due to inflation or growth.
- Identify per pupil costs for major areas of instruction, services, and student activities. Per pupil costs are easier to grasp and compare than total program budget figures.
- Prepare "visuals" (graphs, charts, tables, transparencies, PowerPoint presentations, etc.) for presentation to study groups and the general public.
- Pool recommendations from all sources and prepare an administrative recommendation to the school board; present the recommendations to the board at a well-publicized meeting that occurs sometime prior to the finalization of the budget that will be presented to the board and budget committee at a later time.
- Hold hearings to invite responses from the staff and the general public, then revise original recommendations accordingly.
- Make board decisions at well-publicized meetings. Budget committee members should be included in all presentations to the board; however, the board is responsible for making final decisions.

Involving the staff and community in budgeting has many advantages, and the media are more likely to support budget efforts if it is perceived that a substantial effort has been made to be honest and open. However, staff and community need to be involved early on—not as an afterthought. Merely asking for their reactions once the superintendent's budget recommendations have been presented to the board casts doubt on the district's sincerity in involving staff and community.

In this regard, follow-up is also important—those involved want to know how their recommendations were acted upon. Letting them know that their involvement is valued builds support for the district.

### Examining Cost-cutting Alternatives

The next order of business is to examine available alternatives. Measures that have been taken by school districts and other public service agencies tend to fall into a pattern, ranging from most to least desirable:

Level 1. *Increase productivity.* The district may decide to enlarge class sizes, coordinate or consolidate similar functions within the district or with other districts (in such areas as purchasing, transportation, or media programs), use computer-assisted instruction, two-way, interactive video, Internet courses, satellite TV, correspondence, or other distance-learning technologies to meet certain instructional needs, economize (on supplies, electricity, etc.) or in other ways bring about greater cost effectiveness.

Level 2. *Defer spending.* The district may "make do" for the time being on such matters as maintenance, capital outlay, or textbook purchases. These decisions must be made with care, to avoid expenses in the future that would be unnecessary if sound preventative measures were to be taken now.

Level 3. *Reduce services by cutting program budgets equally.* "Across the board" reductions in spending might be sufficient to solve the budget problems; each program administrator would be required to find a way to cut back a given percentage—somewhere. By spreading relatively small cuts across the entire organization, nearly the same level of quality can be maintained.

Level 4. *Eliminate "nonessential" services.* Rather than force deeper cuts across all programs, a district may decide to do without certain programs or services altogether. Certain athletic programs, staff support services, school food service, student transportation, and so forth might fall into this category.

*Level 5. Eliminate or drastically reduce positions, programs, and services.* After most other options have been exhausted, professional staff reduction remains as a last resort. Options to consider include voluntary agreement to take unpaid furloughs, early retirement, reducing the work week to four days, eliminating staff positions, or in some other way trimming salary costs. Other severe alternatives are consolidation with another district, school closure, and instructional program elimination.

The above measures are not meant to be taken sequentially in every case (i.e., first exhausting all options in level 1, then moving on to level 2, etc.). Neither should all programs necessarily be reduced in the same manner (i.e., applying level 5 measures equally across all instructional programs). When deciding where and how deeply to cut, the following factors should be considered:

- The total budget savings required to balance anticipated income and expenditures;
- The long-term expectations for federal, state, and local revenues;
- The district's history of cost-cutting measures that already have been implemented in each program area;
- The impact of future budget cuts on program effectiveness; and
- Priorities expressed by the board, administration, staff, and community regarding the importance of each program area.

The need to consider the first factor is clear and has already been discussed, to some extent, earlier in this chapter; however, the need to weigh the remaining four factors is discussed below.

*Long-term Revenue Projections.* Recalling our earlier discussion, districts will vary in their projections of long-term financial health. For example, districts, which foresee a short-term deficit, necessitating immediate expenditure cuts, but who anticipate an eventual return to current revenues in the long run, might rely on level 2 (deferred spending) alternatives. Another district, one with little expectation of future budget restorations, might emphasize level 3 (across the board) options. Similarly, when it comes to cutting staff positions, this same district may decide to abolish positions that can be reestablished without extensive training and orientation or that can be easily filled. If declining resources are likely to be a continuing problem, such considerations are not as relevant. Again, this thinking also applies to programs—other factors being equal, those programs that can be rebuilt more easily without sacrificing quality might be cut first; those that would take years to reestablish might be protected.

The district's long-term financial picture also might affect the number of cost-cutting alternatives that are considered. For example, if a district expects deficits over the next two or three years, budget cuts beyond those needed to balance the coming year's budget should be analyzed. In this manner, for example, if reduction-in-staff is decided upon, savings might be compounded over three years rather than one by making this difficult decision now. Attention should be focused on reductions needed for the duration—not only as an exercise in contingency planning but also to help guide current budget deliberations. Some programs may be able to absorb successive budget cuts better than others; that is, there may be programs that might have to be cut completely due to the fact that their entire effectiveness depends on maintaining funding at the present level. Or, if such a program is essential, it might best be spared with incremental reductions applied to other program areas.

The danger in basing budget decisions on the long-term financial outlook is that revenue projections might be inaccurate. The legislature may decide to alter the method of financing public schools or the economy may recover faster than expected. A long-term projection applied to current costs and revenues is only one of many factors to be considered.

*Prior Budget Cuts.* The district's history of cost-cutting measures directly affects current alternatives. If the district already has used the first three levels of options described earlier, the only recourse may be to eliminate programs and staff. After two or three years of budget cutting, the original set of priorities may have been forgotten, and a new set, reflected in the reduced budget, may have become the norm. Some programs or services may have been reduced more than others, and if this is not acknowledged, additional cuts may not reflect the policies in effect when retrenchment began.

*Impact on Program Effectiveness.* There are a number of ways to estimate the potential impact of cuts on the quality and effectiveness of school programs. "Cutback impact statements" can help to organize information, including opinions and perceptions, about the consequences of a given reduction, showing clearly what is being sacrificed. An impact statement might include:

• A general description of the cutback proposal;
• The number of students involved and how they are affected;
• The number of staff involved and how they are affected;
• The consequences (advantages and disadvantages);
• Possible effect on other programs or services;
• Legal implications (e.g., regarding state standards, handicapped laws, etc.); and
• Dollars saved. (Hefty 1981, 241)

Another useful impact statement format includes these suggestions from Oliver Brown, assistant superintendent for business management services at the time in Cambridge, Massachusetts. He suggests the following structure for all reports and impact statements going to the school board:

Start with an introduction: purpose, scope, problems. Then include:

1. Summary and Recommendations
2. Current Problems, Policy, Practice and Costs
3. Alternative Policies, Practices and Costs
4. Comparative Analysis of Alternative Benefits, Effects, Costs
5. Rationale for Recommendations
6. Implementation Alternatives
7. Recommended Implementation Plan Including Tasks, Responsibilities, and a Timetable,
8. Conclude with appendices[1]

The cost-saving ideas included in chapters 2 through 5 of this book present general impact statements regarding selected cost-cutting measures. In a district's own impact analyses, either one of the above formats might be followed, utilizing more specific information particular to your district, or you may wish to develop your own format.

---

1. (Reprinted with permission, from The American School Board Journal, October 1978. Copyright 1978, the National School Boards Association. All Rights Reserved. Article entitled, "Pages and pages on how to cut school costs—wisely," p. 36.)

*Priorities*. Setting priorities lies at the heart of the matter in adjusting school budgets. (Several dated but still excellent articles have addressed priority-setting issues. See, for example, Doherty, V. and J. Fenwick, "Can Budget Reduction be Rational?" *Educational Leadership* 39, no. 4 (January 1982): 252–57.) The board's policies on overall educational goals for the district can serve as a starting point from which more specific priorities can be developed. Other avenues for setting priorities include the following: (1) conduct community and staff surveys, asking for ranking of specific cost-cutting alternatives; (2) seek wide citizen and staff participation in discussing and recommending cuts to the superintendent and budget committee; and (3) examine available needs assessment data.

## Presenting Options to the Board of Directors

The superintendent and budget committee must weigh the alternatives available and present them to the board. The following information should be included:

- An impact statement that indicates the consequences of eliminating a given item;
- The amount of money saved;
- The superintendent's rationale for recommending the items for elimination;
- Recommendations of study groups or advisory committees; and
- Any relevant survey or needs assessment data.

## Evaluating the Impact of Budget Reduction

The study of changes in program effectiveness and productivity following budget cuts will provide useful information for future budget decisions. Ideally, the district should keep baseline data on key indicators of school effectiveness and productivity. Knowing about changes in such indicators will be helpful in decision making. Districts may wish to share ideas, data-collection instruments and processes, sample evaluation studies, and templates for presenting data to the school board, staff, local community members, legislators, and tips on using evaluation data in the budgeting process.

# 2

## Cost-saving Tips for District and School-level Administration

District and school administrators are taking steps to reduce costs and balance their budgets, some of which are listed here. In the next few years, it may become necessary to reconsider a number of short- and long-range measures that, until now, have been used only selectively. Ideas to consider include:

### DISTRICT ADMINISTRATION

1. Recover more of the direct costs for such programs as school lunch, interschool activities, special electives, adult education, and evening activities.
2. Extend the school day and reduce the week to four or four and one-half days. (No substitutes for coaches.)
3. Reduce the number of administrators through multiassignment.
4. Organize schedules so that specialized staff can work in two or more buildings.
5. Develop a well-planned reduction-in-force policy that will allow for the transfer of staff to improve pupil-teacher ratios in specialized areas.
6. In larger districts with multiple schools, consider closing school buildings not needed. Research, develop criteria, establish procedures for closure, and strategically plan for the management of conflict and political backlash that comes with school closure in many cases.

27

## BUSINESS

To obtain the best possible value for each taxpayer's dollar, districts could contract for services. However, if the district staff can provide a service at a lower cost, a contract would not be warranted.

1. Contracting Services. Responsibility for building and grounds maintenance, food service operations, transportation, custodial services, insurance, computer applications and technology support, etc., can be considered for private contracting, or obtained through education service districts.

   - Prepare bidding specifications carefully.
   - Prepare cost studies for use in making cost comparisons.
   - Termination clauses provide protection from poor service or loss in financial support as a result of levy failures, or federal/state revenue reductions.
   - The district's labor agreements must allow for such contracting.

2. Insurance. Money often can be saved by bidding for insurance, and almost all types of insurance can be bid successfully.

   - Prepared specifications are key to successful bidding.
   - Consultants can help reduce risks, losses, and costs.
   - Be sure that insurance possibilities are not restricted by employee bargaining agreements.
   - Local agents and firms should not be given preference.
   - Some districts (or a consortium) may consider self-insurance.

3. Computers. Computerization of business services can cut costs and increase efficiency if implemented correctly.

   - Computers for business can be used to some degree by districts of any size.
   - Many good business software packages complete with tech support services are available to most districts at reasonable costs.
   - Beware of software limitations and how the particular software you are considering meshes with state and federal reporting requirements and forms to be submitted electronically before buying or leasing any data processing hardware.

- The computer programs developed by some districts for scheduling transportation maintenance have improved cost effectiveness.

4. Improve the management of cash flow from all sources.

- Lower the number of "idle fund" days.
- Increase cash flow monitoring (minicomputers, charts).
- Improve investment policies and practices.
- Demand district money held by the county.

5. Increase cooperative business functions; decrease the number of staff working on business functions. Watch for duplicate accounting systems in district programs.

6. Expand the use of regional purchasing for supplies, equipment, and vehicles.

- Use disposable items (mops, filters, etc.).

7. Establish a multiyear capital improvement plan.

- What can be put off now?
- What will the costs be later if the scheduled protective maintenance or project is put off now?

8. Look to the various business task force on education recommendations available from your state's local lobbying group for business as a resource.

    *Note:* The Public Contract Review Board rules in your state apply to the sale of public property just as they do to purchasing. As an example, in Oregon, for any item valued at $500 or more, a district must try to obtain three quotes; on items less than $500, quotes are encouraged.

## PERSONNEL

### Ideas That Increase Revenue, Productivity, or Efficiency

1. Utilize staff development and training to prepare current employees for new or added responsibilities.

- Train district staff to serve in staff development roles.
- Train teachers for new positions by providing in-service, graduate course reimbursement, and so forth.

2. Invite bargaining units to participate in cost cutting through "quality circles"—small groups of employees who meet to discuss work and identify ways to become more productive.
3. Develop a well-planned reduction-in-force policy whereby staff members can be transferred to improve pupil-teacher ratios in specialized areas.
4. Stagger building schedules so that specialized staff can work in two or more buildings and students can be transported more efficiently.
5. Combine two or more part-time positions into one full-time position.
6. When an additional class section is needed in a secondary school, pay a regular teacher to work an extra period rather than hiring a teacher for that period.
7. Hire two or three "permanent substitutes" to replace absent staff members. This may provide for better substitute service.
8. Place all administrators on eight-hour day, twelve-month contracts.
9. Extend the working day for consultants.
10. Redescribe staff responsibilities.

   - Analyze job descriptions for cooks, custodians, bus drivers, and others.
   - Utilize a high school librarian for district-wide purchasing of library/media services.
   - Employ out-of-district consultants to complete specific, one-time tasks at a cost less than maintaining a full-time staff person with those skills.
   - Select teachers to coordinate curriculum development projects on a part-time basis.
   - Utilize substitute teacher funds for such enrichment programs as films, guest speakers, and so on. An absent teacher could elect either a substitute teacher for the class or enrichment program attendance.
   - Expand the duties of teacher aides and paraprofessionals to the full extent allowed by law and regulations.
   - Use paraprofessionals for study hall or corridor duty, allowing teachers more time for instruction.

- Change staffing patterns; replace an all-teacher physical educa-tion staff with a team made up of fewer teachers and more trained paraprofessionals for less pay.
11. Utilize volunteers for tutoring, grading papers, and other services.
12. Hire employees in cooperation with other agencies, such as other school districts, education service districts, community colleges, city and county government, state department of human resources, and so forth.
13. Reduce staff absenteeism (cutting health costs) by initiating or im-proving an employee wellness program. Contact your insurance agent of record for details.
14. Develop a secretarial pool of hours for each school. In the elemen-tary schools, for example, they have peak periods such as the start of school, grading periods, the end of school, and so on. Each school could be provided with a pool of hours that they could draw upon whenever they wish to use them.

## Ideas That Reduce Expenditures without Necessarily Reducing Services

1. Develop collective bargaining contracts carefully.

- Do not tie salary increases directly to the Consumer Price Indexes; this may result in an escalation of salaries beyond the funds available.
- Sign a two- or three-year agreement with employees, but provide for a review of the economic package for the second and third years.
- Renegotiate salary schedules.
- Freeze or reduce all salaries for a specified period of time.
- Hold to the same salary schedule for another year, but allow the step increases on the salary schedule to remain.
- Hold the same salary schedule for another year, but negotiate a to-tal freeze including the step increase.
- Review and standardize salary and fringe benefit programs for all employees, eliminating costly exceptions.

- Coordinate fringe benefits (medical and major medical, dental, vision, and life insurance) in cases where both spouses work for the school district.
- Provide insurance coverage only for the employee.
- Negotiate for increases in fringe benefits in lieu of salary increases.
- Negotiate fringe benefit dollars, not benefits.
- Districts paying insurance premiums for teachers could initiate a wellness insurance plan, with a portion of premiums returned to each member who stays well.
- Freeze or reduce tuition reimbursement allowances.
- Freeze or reduce paid leaves.

2. Review personnel policies for possible savings. Consider such factors as staff development activities, professional growth requirements, pay policies.

3. Implement a plan requiring that school district administrators develop specific written suggestions to reduce costs, and to improve efficiency and productivity. This could be done on a quarterly basis and included as a part of their performance evaluation.

4. Reduce the need for substitute teachers by minimizing teacher absenteeism. For example, one district removed its ceiling on accumulated sick leave, which significantly reduced absenteeism because employees knew that they would not "lose" sick leave hours.

5. Use temporary contracts for all new employees.

6. Hold off some teacher hiring until the start of the school year if elementary class sizes are not definite.

7. Hire personnel according to midyear enrollment projections (which tend to be lower) rather than projections for the beginning of the school year.

8. Conduct all in-service during nonschool hours or on Saturdays.

9. Encourage all classes of employees to take early retirement by providing cash bonus or retroactive pay raise incentives. Provide early retirees with part-time employment opportunities. Increased staff turnover saves the dollar difference between top and entry-level salary schedules.

10. Adopt assertive termination procedures for those who cannot provide satisfactory services. In times of staff reduction, this could help retain excellent teachers who may be less experienced.

## Ideas That Reduce Expenditures by Reducing Services

1. Determine whether the district is overstaffed and reduce staff where possible.

   • Employ fewer specialists (music, physical education, special education, and so forth).
   • Reduce the number of sections offered at the secondary school level.
   • Contract with a community college for advanced courses.
   • Shift or combine assignments.

2. Freeze hiring or establish a strict review process for hiring new employees to replace those leaving.

   • Do not replace personnel who have taken leaves of absence.

3. Reduce the number of administrators through multiassignments.

   • Share an area specialist with other districts.
   • Assign one principal to two schools, with a vice-principal or head teacher in each school.
   • Assign principals to teach part time.
   • Establish combined superintendent/principal positions.
   • Combine curriculum supervision with evaluation supervision.

4. Decentralize district administration; eliminate district curriculum departments and replace them with assignments to school administrators and staff.

5. Reduce the need for substitute teachers by utilizing administrators and counselors in the classrooms (e.g., each administrator and counselor in the district might be required to serve in the classroom for three days during the year).

6. Assign one fewer substitute per day to each high school (e.g., eight teacher absences, seven substitutes).

7. Utilize classroom teacher/student advisors to supplement the high school counseling program.

8. Where possible, reduce full-time teaching and nonteaching positions to half time (e.g., librarian, home economics, foreign language).

9. Eliminate the number of specialist teachers with formal teaching loads and use them as resource teachers to assist regular classroom teachers.

## SCHOOL-LEVEL ADMINISTRATION

School administrators and staff members provide direct services to students, and it is their responsibility to protect the health and safety of students while providing quality instruction. All of this should be done in a cost-effective manner, and school principals are now challenged to find ways to economize further. Staff and students can provide valuable suggestions. Everyone should understand that some areas facing cutbacks will be reinstated when funds allow, while other changes actually may prove to be better than current approaches.

Some of the matters for consideration are:

- Establish criteria for setting priorities.
- Consider ways to handle disruptive students and handicapped students. Perhaps compulsory attendance rules need modification.
- Be prepared to respond to the claim that the "senior year" is a waste.
- Research ways to modify building schedules, keeping parent and student complaints to a minimum.
- Consider alternative energy sources and ways to economize.
- Find ways to deal with collective bargaining requirements.
- Find out if your state's Teachers Standards and Practices Commission will modify rules or grant waivers on assignments.

The following money-saving suggestions focus on the use of staff and the school schedule; many can be found in other sections of this publication as well (e.g., chapter 3, Cost-saving Tips for Instructional Services). The idea is to develop class and building schedules that provide for more cost-effective programs and services.

### Staff

1. Consider contract alternatives used by some districts.

    - Reduce the number of days in contracts for administrators, teachers, and nonteaching staff (e.g., from 190 days to 187).
    - Add vacation days without pay.
    - Assign one certificated position to a program, assisted by volunteers and minimum-pay personnel.

- Cut back on the number of certificated supervisors.
- Utilize more part-time personnel.
- Utilize retired personnel more effectively.
- Contract with community college staff or part-time teachers to teach specialized courses at the junior or senior high school level where there is limited enrollment or a lack of staff expertise.
- Increase the use of student work programs.
- Assign fewer coaches per sport.
- Avoid duplication of classes offered at the middle and senior high schools.
- Analyze the need for temporary employees. Consider consolidating part-time functions into full-time positions; temporary employees can help with short-term needs.

2. Consider cost-saving measures that may involve a request for a waiver of the state standards for public schools.

- Cut back on the number of days of instruction in the classroom by assigning students to outside research projects and individual study programs (field trips and similar programs).
- Utilize a four-day workweek, with longer school days and additional work assignments.
- Delay purchasing textbooks if current programs are successful now; the state may be willing to grant independent adoptions or waivers.

3. Reduce extracurricular activities.

- Assign a minimum of one female, one male, and one coed activity in both the athletic and nonathletic areas for each quarter (fall, winter, spring).
- Reduce interschool activity schedules, including the number of activities, nonleague activities, and tournaments, and distances traveled.
- Encourage more home activities and organize fundraisers to raise funds to offset the cost of the activity.

4. Reduce the number of electives. Consider scheduling a six-period day rather than seven periods.

5. Increase class size on a selective basis.
6. Offer driver training during the summer only on a self-supporting tuition basis.

## Building Schedules

1. Examine subject matter content and methods, and consider combining all three major high school science courses (biology, chemistry, physics) into a single integrated course that is scheduled over a three-year period, resulting in increased class size, fewer sections, and better use of science rooms and labs.
2. Combine several levels of the same content area into a single class; for example, second-, third-, and fourth-year foreign language classes could be taught during the same period.
3. Consider the twelve-month school year.

   - Beneficial in a period of growth in student population.
   - Added operating costs (custodial, administrative).
   - Seems most acceptable to parents and students in lower grades.

4. Consider a daily class schedule that places all planning time at the beginning of each day; teachers then are available for assignment during class time.

## Transportation

Develop transportation patterns to reduce routes and frequency.

1. In districts with large numbers of students and a comparatively small geographical size, stagger class starting and dismissal times to better utilize drivers and buses. The district will spend less on equipment, storage areas, insurance, and drivers' wages, benefits, training, and licensing. One large suburban district has found that its buses could be reduced almost 20 percent by rerouting, and by staggering the elementary school schedules by one-half hour.
2. Smaller districts with large distances to cover could eliminate early afternoon routes for the primary grades. While staff and parents may protest the longer school day, there will be cost savings.

3. Increase the walking distance expected of students to school and bus stops. While many believe this to be the best way to cut costs, it has proven to be highly controversial. Care must be taken to avoid possible traffic hazards to students.
4. Evaluate bus routes to be sure that buses are not duplicating one another, and that bus loading is distributed for greatest efficiency.
5. Reduce deadhead mileage by adding bus storage areas.
6. Stagger building schedules so that specialized staff can work in two or more buildings, and students can be transported more efficiently.
7. Reduce the frequency of early dismissals that require additional bus runs; dismiss all students at the same time to reduce runs.
8. Consider implementing "pod" or "clustered pickup points" for picking up or letting off students instead of offering door-to-door transportation.

## Staffing Patterns

1. Study staff assignments to minimize "misassignments," but when necessary, plan appropriate in-service programs to assist in shifting employees to new assignments.
2. Develop and use a current catalog of graduates, retired employees, and others in the community who may be willing to supplement instructional activities.
3. Develop, implement, and encourage a program designed to make use of community volunteers.

## Use of Buildings

1. Study buildings to make full use of all school facilities, including multipurpose and other instructional spaces.
2. Close wings or units of buildings by consolidating space.
3. Develop safety consciousness to reduce state accident insurance fund fees.
4. Consider setting up a fund for student activities that is used to pay for vandalism, with the balance available for student use.
5. Establish a realistic fee schedule for use of buildings by outside groups to at least recover the energy and custodial costs.

## EXPANDED COST-SAVING IDEAS

### Expanded Idea #1

Negotiate the "real cost to district" for wages and related costs, rather than just for "increases in salary schedule." In most districts, advertised salary increases are below the actual cost for those increases. For example, when the district provides a cost-of-living increase in salary schedules and pays increased insurance premiums as well, the district is, in effect, paying insurance costs twice.

*Advantage:* Focuses on total employee compensation—all fixed charges and fringe benefit costs [i.e., PERS, Public Employee Retirement System, contribution (both employer and 6 percent pickup)], Social Security, workers' compensation, sick leave, vacation leave, as well as insurance premiums.

*Disadvantage:* Probably will be resisted by employees.

*Additional Information:* It is helpful to list proposed schedules and projected total costs to the district.

Previous year's real cost to district = $_____

Percentage proposed salary increase x previous year's cost =

_____

Plus increases in workers' compensation, increases in Social Security insurance, increases in retirement (PERS), and increases in any other fringe benefits _____

Dollars needed to increase scheduled amounts = $_____

### Expanded Idea #2

*Case Study Example: Pilot Rock School District, Pilot Rock, Oregon:* Reward the entire staff for participating in a "wellness" program by offering an insurance rebate, such as Blue Cross's "wellcheck," or by allowing staff to exercise during certain prescribed times.

*Advantages:* May increase productivity (better morale, less absenteeism, better instruction); helps inform the community about wellness; may save money for the district; may increase student/staff attendance.

*Disadvantage:* The community will need to be informed.

*Additional Information:* In-service programs may be needed about wellness, with an informed staff member to monitor the program.

**Expanded Idea #3**

Utilize current staff members as resource personnel for in-service training. A peer training model was introduced in one district when a full-time position for training special educators was lost. Using new state performance requirement standards for teaching, the district developed its own standards as well as a self-analysis system. Staff members assessed their own skills in light of the new standards and identified areas where they felt that they needed in-service. Then staff trainers with expertise in those areas developed specific training modules.

*Advantages:* Groups with like needs plan their own in-services and select district personnel who have the skills to deliver training; staff participate in setting their own goals; peer trainers tend to become aware of district policies and practices; the trainers can be called on over an extended period of time; training can be conducted as part of (or in place of) staff meetings; teachers from different disciplines are brought together, allowing for cross training among disciplines; a district staff development person is not needed to manage the program; the system allows staff members to make use of their special skills; it focuses on particular skills needed throughout the district; and expenses for outside-district trainers are saved.

*Disadvantages:* It may be difficult to agree on a time and place for personnel to meet (one district scheduled a monthly three-hour staff meeting and training session in its contract); some teachers may find it difficult to accept training from their peers; there may be areas of need that cannot be addressed by current staff.

*Additional Information:* While peer trainers can save money, trainers are only a part of a larger, well-organized system that must be in place. If experts are needed to provide specific training in addition to peer training, they may be contracted on an hourly basis.

**Administrative Cost-saving Case Study Examples**

Many smaller school districts that once enjoyed a full complement of administrators are finding it necessary to move toward the superintendent/principal concept as the administrative staff becomes thinner.

Several years ago, one area school district found itself in just such a situation with a shortage of administrative help and a variety of administrative duties that needed doing. Instead of hiring additional regular administrative help—which the budget precluded—the district looked at some of the primary duties that had been carried out by the principal and created several positions such as activities and athletic director, testing and assessment coordinator, and attendance coordinator. The district provided a stipend for each assignment and enlisted some young teachers eager for a pay boost to take on the tasks.

The district was able to get some of its administrative tasks done much more economically, enhance the pay of some struggling new teachers, and provide them with some expanded career experiences.

Other districts are moving toward internal consolidation in terms of reducing the number of building sites they operate. This provides for more efficient use of principals and for administrative support personnel.

Some other districts are contracting for administrative oversight through other school districts or regional service agencies. Contracting for a part-time superintendent often provides a level of expertise for some tasks that a district might not otherwise be able to experience if it were to try providing its own administrator.

When its superintendent retired, the Grant Education Service District contracted with the North Central ESD (Educational School District) for superintendent services. Now the NCESD superintendent travels to Grant County several times a month to provide administrative leadership.

## Association of Educational Purchasing Agencies Case Study Example

There are twenty-one regional service agencies across the United States that have joined together to form a national purchasing cooperative that offers both bid support and considerable cost savings, called the AEPA (Association of Educational Purchasing Agencies) Purchasing Cooperative.

This cooperative was founded to create lower prices, provide greater leverage in dealing with vendor problems, and allows the dollars saved through such a venture to be used for classroom instruction.

One of the attributes of the cooperative is that it often delivers the goods and services through local distributors or dealers. This cooperative provides a wide variety of purchasing possibilities including:

- Playground equipment
- Roofing

- Portables
- School specialty supplies
- Computer supplies
- Library books
- Athletic equipment
- Athletic field and track surfacing
- Administrative software

A list of the individual, regional members of the AEPA School Purchasing Cooperative can be found in appendix A.

## Cost-savings Example: Employee Benefits

One of the attractions of working in public education has always been the existence of health, dental, and vision benefits. At a time when school support is often stagnant or extremely limited, the costs of such benefit plans have begun rising at the rate of 10 to 15 percent per year. As this is being written, a quality medical benefit plan is running in the $800 to $900 per month range or perhaps more. And as a result, benefits are becoming a much greater part of overall compensation and employment costs—so much so, that education employers are beginning to look seriously at other options. Some of these include:

- A natural first consideration is higher deductibles and less comprehensive benefit plans, which are constantly being explored by districts.
- Other districts and even entire states or regions are beginning to look seriously at alternative approaches to their traditional carriers.
- Still others are looking very seriously at what once might have been relatively innocuous contract provisions providing generous benefits for part-time employees. In some cases, that has included the possibility of full coverage for those working half time or more.
- Benefits have become so much a part of the growing cost of maintaining regular employees that districts are looking at contracting or other employment or staff utilization models that reduce exposure to benefit obligations.
- Where allowable, some districts are providing incentives for employees to consider other alternatives. For example, in one district

that provides fully paid medical, there was no disincentive for dual-employed family members to only take one plan. The district decided to offer a $250 monthly TSA (tax shelter annuity) for any staff member who did not sign up for the medical benefit. The district saved approximately $7,200 per year, per employee.

- In another district that paid a sizeable portion of the medical benefit, a similar incentive was offered to dual-employee family members. The difference between the district's contribution and the full cost was approximately $150. For families where both the husband and wife were employed by the district, the extra $150 was paid by the district, which essentially provided that family with fully paid medical. Had both the husband and wife taken the medical benefits, the cost to the district could have been another $550 per month.

## CREATIVE COST-SAVINGS CASE STUDY EXAMPLE: IONE SCHOOL DISTRICT, IONE, OREGON

Ione is a small community of 332 residents located in southern Morrow County (Oregon). Faced with the possibility of losing their high school, the residents launched a vigorous attempt to form their own small district and break off from the county unit. A well-organized lobbying effort resulted in success at the state legislature and the Ione Self-Determination Committee suddenly found itself with a district of its own. Ione had, for fifty years, been part of the Morrow County School District with a countywide population of 2,300 students. Now they were a district of 160 students with a legislative charter but no real means to operate a school district.

Shortly after the legislature granted permission to Ione, they were cut adrift from the Morrow County School District. This took place in mid-June. Without a board of their own or any type of governance structure, they came under the guidance of the Umatilla-Morrow Education Service District. Several school leaders in Ione had suggested that if the district were to sustain itself, it would need to have a whole new look in terms of organization. By mid-July, a new five-member board was in place in Ione. But during the intervening month, leaders from the Ione community and the ESD had already been involved in discussions about options for creating a new management structure focused on sustainability and reduced operating costs.

Both groups agreed that there are several fundamental issues at work in rural districts that have caused them to resist consolidation efforts and remain independent. These include the need to have a local board in place representing community interests. It also, of course, includes having a school in the community to preserve a town's identity. And it includes having an extracurricular activities program as a focus for community interest and participation. These are the visible signs of local control. Who transports the students to and from school, who feeds them, who provides staff development, who pays the bills and keeps the school in good repair, and who deals with a myriad of complex reporting requirements is negotiable and not of high-profile public interest.

In October 2002, the Oregon Department of Education Office of School Finance, Data, and Analysis produced a report on the costs of operating small schools in Oregon. Commissioned by the Interim Legislative Committees on Education, the report was designed to provide both an analysis of the costs of operating small schools and suggestions for more efficient practices. That report advised that strategies should be developed with ESDs to increase the efficiency of operating small schools. The report also suggested that spreading fixed costs more effectively through the use of an ESD model might be one answer. The report also specifically pointed to large-group purchasing of supplies, equipment, and services as another potential model for cost savings. All of these suggestions have been incorporated into the Ione Model and in subsequent models that have now been expanded to other districts.

As one individual, now a member of the Ione board stated, "We want to become a model for how small, rural districts in Oregon and elsewhere can survive. We have the unique opportunity of building our district from the ground up and we can structure that process around finding ways to do business differently."

One of the first new approaches was to turn to the Education Service District for management services in literally every area except actual classroom instruction. During the 2003–2004 school year, the district even contracted for a superintendent although they maintained a site administrator. In 2004–2005 they will employ a superintendent/principal, although the ESD will continue to provide some level of mentorship and management oversight. Some of the areas of contracting include:

- The district has no deputy clerk—all business functions including payroll are handled by the ESD; the site administrator and building secretary code purchase orders and send them on the ESD. Most regular bills, such as utilities, go directly to the ESD—as does the basic revenue.
- The ESD is the personnel office for Ione, including recruitment, selection, contract management, and negotiations.
- The ESD manages all technology functions.
- The ESD contracts for food service and maintenance/custodial services.
- The district contracts with a private carrier for transportation.
- The ESD provides all curriculum, testing, and assessment, and staff development services.
- The ESD Special Education director also serves in the same capacity for Ione.
- The ESD provides printing and purchasing services.
- Ione has an administrator who, along with the teaching staff, handles daily operations including, of course, instruction.
- A multimillion-dollar building project was underway when the district was formed and the ESD contracted for oversight services to assure the project was completed properly.

The district contracts with the City of Ione to mow and water its athletic field. The city has purchased a new $30,000 mower, which it uses for the task. The school district does not own any mowing equipment. The city charges $30 per hour for the job and is able to help amortize its purchase. The district does not have to bear the cost of purchasing the equipment, maintaining the equipment, or paying someone to operate it.

At a presentation on the new model, one board member told the audience that the district "now has the largest central office staff of any district of its size in the America." While it only has parts of central office staff, the district has access to levels of expertise and specialization not generally available in the operation of small districts. For example, the district pays $6,000 per year for personnel services. In return, it has access to three full-time human resource professionals who oversee recruitment and selection, negotiations, contract management, benefits, and similar complex matters. The district pays $4,000 per year for a director of special education who handles oversight of all special education reporting, audits, and similar issues. The technology management contract of $15,000 per year includes access to a staff of more than fifty individuals and includes desktop support, network analysts, web page development and maintenance, and the oversight of the required technology plan. Having just one individual in the district to handle technology under the old model would have cost $40,000 to $50,000. For assessment and testing, curriculum services, technology in the classroom, and staff development coordination, the district pays $5,000 per year. In return, it has access to a staff of more than twenty professionals.

Like all districts in the ESD, Ione is entitled to a certain menu of basis "Resolution Services." The specific services noted above are well beyond those that would be routinely provided. Because of Ione's limited staff, the board has formed two major committees: the Buildings and Grounds Committee, which oversees maintenance as well as long-range needs, and the Student Success Committee, which deals with a variety of ways to expand services to students and improve both staff development and student achievement.

The Buildings and Grounds Committee, working with the same consultant used to oversee the completion of the construction project, prepared a four-page list of every conceivable item that needed to be addressed anywhere on the school grounds in terms of maintenance or repair. The list was then divided up among the two custodians, the members of the Buildings and Grounds Committee, community volunteers, and specialized workers. During the holiday break, a seven-member team (including the above individuals) started down the list. While they didn't get to the bottom, they made dramatic headway. This same consultant has been maintained on a long-term basis to return to the district once or twice each year to evaluate maintenance and custodial activities and make suggestions regarding this area.

While the district cannot afford the services of a counselor, it has contracted with a specialist who comes one day a week to work with students having behavior issues. Other counseling duties such as helping students schedule themselves or prepare for college are handled by the Student

Success Committee. This committee often calls upon recent graduates to assist students with their transition to higher education and to meet with younger students to provide guidance in early course selection.

Through its contract with the ESD, the district discovered that it was eligible for Title funds and received approximately $50,000 that had not previously been available. This permitted the creation of a summer school as well as daily remediation efforts focused on mathematics and reading. At the same time, the Ione Education Foundation decided it would like to encourage the restoration of music in the schools. The foundation agreed to provide funding for a half-time music teacher. The district was then able to engage a half-time music, half-time Title teacher. In such a rural area, it would have been difficult if not impossible to find a half-time teacher in either area.

In the Ione model, the staff was reduced by three teaching periods to create revenues for online instruction. The fiscal value of the three teaching periods is more than enough to cover the costs of all online courses that might be needed by students. Aides at the school are being used for monitoring the online learning. Much the same is happening with technology. While the district is required to maintain oversight from a licensed librarian, no such person exists in Morrow County—either in the Ione District or the Morrow County District. As a result, Ione has contracted with a licensed individual from the Milton-Freewater School District who will contribute fifteen days per year working with the library aide on media skills, analyzing the collection, working with teachers to develop strategies for incorporating library resources into the classroom, and developing orders for materials. While this solution provides the district with access to professional oversight for its library program, the daily management of the library remains with an aide who doubles as the overseer for online learning since distance education facilities are a part of the library facility.

On the last day of school before the holiday break in December 2003, members of the school board distributed gourmet hams to every staff member in the district to recognize their contributions to the children of Ione. The hams were a gift from various factions in the community. A week earlier, the board had traveled to Pendleton to present gift boxes of fruit to sixteen ESD staff members who had helped get the district off the ground. They also presented these individuals with a holiday wreath—all part of the board's genuine commitment to the development of a highly positive and progressive learning environment that reflects much different working conditions than those normally experienced these days by public educators. It isn't just the funding model that has changed in Ione, it is the entire school climate and the relationship between the community and its schools.

This is by no means the answer for every district, but there are principles in this organizational plan that have merit for consideration in other districts. There is a five-member board in Ione that provides a strong measure of local control. No one in the district has raised an issue with who is paying the bills or handling the myriad of other details surrounding the management of the school district. They have confirmed that they fundamentally care who is teaching their children and what they are being taught. And they have devised a strategy for retaining their local identity. In fact, during the past year, a wonderful relationship has blossomed between the ESD staff and the Ione community. Those staff members who visit regularly are invited to community events and are welcomed when they stop by the local restaurant for a meal.

The contracted superintendent was the guest speaker at commencement and helped distribute diplomas. He was then invited to a variety of post-graduation parties at the homes of students. At the Fourth of July Blues Festival, which is the annual community celebration, it is likely that a large contingent of ESD staff will be in attendance. This was also the case at the end-of-school luncheon celebrating the first year. And it will also likely be the case in September when the Bank of Eastern Oregon sponsors its annual Back to School BBQ celebrating the first day of school. Last year, that event drew about four hundred parents, students, and community members.

In essence, while Ione has been able to become part of something larger, it has also managed to maintain the fundamentals of local control. Part of Ione's success is the fact that the creation of the management model is not just a fiscal equation; it also includes considerable focus on the development of a positive environment and multiple celebrations within the learning community. This positive environment serves as a critical magnet for attracting willing participants. In the Ione example, the district began with the simple premise: "If there were nothing in place, what would you build in the way of a school district that provides the greatest benefit for the students?"

## A STATE WEIGHS IN ON COST-SAVING MEASURES

In May 2004, the Oregon secretary of state released an audit report evaluating spending on support services in K–12 schools. These were defined as administrative costs such as printing, technology, and staff, and specialized student support such as guidance counselors and health care. Much of his motivation came from a billion-dollar state shortfall and the fact that Oregon was leading the nation with its unemployment rate. In addition, the audit followed a December 2002 report that found Oregon spending more on support services than other states, and that if all Oregon districts had spent the average amount in support services, then over $162 million could have been redirected to instruction. In general,

> Secretary of State auditors found that support services varied widely among districts, and that school districts could benefit by sharing more detailed information about methods used to control spending. Some school districts have controlled the cost of support services by joining together to take advantage of economies of scale in purchasing: obtaining grants, donations, and volunteers from the community; and sharing specialized staff between schools or districts. Other states have created statewide systems for sharing information about successful and cost-effective educational programs.

In terms of finding assistance, the audit spoke of computer donations, the creation of education foundations, and finding additional sources of funding to pay for instructional and other school programs. (In both the Ione and Heppner schools, the licensed staff is augmented by individuals provided through local education foundations).

### Reasons for Higher Costs

The audit revealed widely varied expenditures for support services in similar-sized districts. The districts that had notably higher spending in one or all of the three support categories (business and other support services, student support, and school-level administration) provided the following reasons justifying these higher costs:

- More negotiations of early retirement agreements and increases to the amount of insurance contributions to the supplemental retirement program. (In Oregon, it is not unusual for districts to have special provisions that are paid to employees after retirement, including continuing insurance coverage or other supplemental income based upon service.)

- Location of the district (remoteness/distance).
- Cost to maintain technology originally purchased with grant funds.
- Socioeconomic status of the area (e.g., poverty rate, adult literacy rate, and mobility rate).
- Student population characteristics (e.g., declining enrollment and special education needs for students).
- Determined need for certain levels of school administration (e.g., a full-time principal at a school or directors of student achievement).
- Higher than average staff compensation or staff tenure.

## Successful Strategies for Savings

On the other hand, districts with notably lower spending identified some of the factors they felt contributed to savings:

- Using economies of scale to lower unit costs.
- Obtaining community, contracted, and shared resources.
- Using proactive management programs.
- Identifying additional sources of revenue.

### Economies of Scale

Several districts from Lane County joined a consortium with other districts to achieve some economies of scale in different areas such as the purchase of technical equipment.

The 37,000-student Salem-Keizer School District, Salem, Oregon, has operated a purchasing cooperative serving many other educational and public entities, which lowers costs through volume discounts. This district spent 12 percent less per student on business and other support services than did comparable systems.

Stanfield School District, Stanfield, Oregon, utilized the Intermountain Purchasing Cooperative operated by the Umatilla-Morrow ESD for purchasing and technical services, which staff indicated helped ensure lower prices. The Stanfield District spent 62 percent less per student on business and other support services than did comparably sized colleagues.

Beaverton School District, Beaverton, Oregon, another district in excess of 35,000 students, operates districtwide contracts that have also resulted in better prices. Beaverton's costs in these areas were 18 percent below the average.

The Gladstone School District reported that it was operating large schools near full capacity. Gladstone was 27 percent below like districts in terms of school-level administration expenditures. A number of districts have sought to close buildings with small enrollments in favor of operating fewer schools with larger numbers of students. While the cost efficiencies make sense, the actual process is often fraught with emotional issues and is not always warmly embraced by individual neighborhoods or service areas.

## Community, Contracted, and Shared Resources

Some districts reported that they used retirees, students, and other volunteers in high schools, instead of hiring district employees. Districts reported that they have been assisted by parents and other school supporters in terms of transporting students, maintaining and improving facilities and grounds, assisting with classroom activities, and even assistance with administrative duties. Districts are becoming more and more inclined to share not just specialists such as counselors, psychologists, and speech pathologists but also regular classroom teachers. And in some cases, they are sharing coaches through athletic cooperatives. The Rainier School District, for example, is sharing a special education teaching position with nearby Clatskanie.

Falls City School District, Falls City, Oregon, which spends 46 percent less per student on business and other support services in districts that were reviewed as part of the audit, contracts with the Polk County Mental Health Office for student and family support and counseling services. The Nyssa School District, Nyssa, Oregon, works with both public and private agencies to secure computers.

In the Morrow County School District, a local recreation district was formed to fund extracurricular activities. Until recently, these funds, combined with gate receipts and pay-to-play fees, were sufficient to fund virtually the entire cost of the extracurricular programs. The addition of a new high school and rising costs and participation levels—coupled with stable funds from the recreation district, will place more burden on the school district in terms of program support. Nonetheless, in a district of 2,300 students, the addition of $350,000 in outside program support is a valuable resource. And the recreation district provides another $80,000 in funding to the Ione School District, which is also located in Morrow County.

Some districts, mainly larger ones, have education foundations that assist with a variety of costs. As independent organizations, these foundations can provide unique assistance to local districts. Foundation assistance has ranged from grants for enrichment programs to additional funds for classroom items, to scholarships for graduating seniors, to management resources such as consultation and personnel training.

In the Portland Public Schools, Portland, Oregon, the education foundation helped buy back contracts for some teachers who were the victims of budget cuts. The foundation also helped with grant applications and funding ballot measures. The Gladstone Foundation also helped with enhancing educational programs. In Heppner, the community foundation is providing half a mathematics teacher. In Ione, the foundation funds a half-time music instructor—the only music instructor in the district. In Crane Union High School District, Crane, Oregon, the Crane Areas Schools Education Foundation, funds a grade 7–12 music program after school.

## Proactive Management Programs

In both the Prairie City and Pine Eagle School Districts in Oregon, the ESD has become the focal point for securing student support services. Both are heavily invested in contracting for services and both have experienced dramatic savings as a result.

In the Eugene School District, Eugene, Oregon, the high costs of behavior management programs have been reduced through a deliberate focus on individual education plans.

The Beaverton School District has reported savings brought about through tighter controls over the allocation and authorization of expenditures. The district has also reexamined the practice of large year-end purchases of goods and services when there is remaining budget capacity.

## ADDITIONAL REVENUE SOURCES

As tight times have emerged, districts are looking at a variety of additional revenue sources. Some of these have included:

- Seeking unusual grants to support district functions that have not normally been supported through this method
- Renting out warehouse space
- Renting unused facilities
- Selling surplus property
- Increasing facility fees and leases
- Specialized contracts for beverage sales
- Fees for athletic participation
- Internal facility consolidation

### Staff Management/Negotiated Agreements

Not all new revenue needs come in the form of additional tax appropriations. Sometimes changing the way districts do business and gleaning savings internally can provide dramatic savings. For example, one might ask, "If this were coming out of my pocket, would I be willing to pay someone $20 an hour to do what I am doing at this moment?" It's a good question and one that staff members ought to ask themselves on a regular basis. Sometimes it isn't always what they like doing that makes sense, it's spending time doing things that maximize their talents and training.

Every organization has several individuals who are constantly overwhelmed by the magnitude of their assignment. Often, it isn't the fundamental workload that is the problem, it's their ability to prioritize and focus their energies on the most pressing issues. In the case of some leaders, it is a matter of becoming comfortable with ambiguity and trusting others. Attention to detail is certainly an admirable quality, but when overdone it can turn into paralysis in terms of productivity.

### Facing Tough Personnel Decisions

Some organizations have fallen into the habit of adding staff rather than making tough personnel decisions. Better staff management is a key to cost savings that some organizations would prefer to ignore while others have found that being lean doesn't always mean less productivity. Facing staff evaluation squarely and being willing to consider personnel changes is clearly the "least fun" of all management tasks. But, adversity can sometimes become a source of opportunity; as public schools tighten their collective belts, it is critical that they seek maximum staff performance— a topic that can be discussed more comfortably when the need to stretch dollars is at its peak.

## Negotiated Agreements

An equally difficult topic is the examination of negotiated agreements and reconsideration of wage and benefit provisions as well as the myriad of tiny compensation agreements that have crept into master contracts. There can sometimes be dozens of these latter agreements that, when taken as a group, can add up to mean real dollars. Often, something that didn't seem like much at the time can suddenly become a major expense.

School district boards and administrators would be well advised to conduct an "audit" of their negotiated agreements and try to put a dollar figure to each item—no matter how insignificant—to become familiar with the full cost of employee compensation. The results can often be rather surprising, if not staggering. The intent of this suggestion is not to promote a widespread epidemic of wage and compensation concessions. Rather, with 80–85 percent of most school district budgets committed to staff costs, it would make sense that this area receive at least as much attention as the usual efforts to slice travel, maintenance, library books, and the other costs that actually make up a rather small percentage of the average school district budget.

# 3

## Cost-saving Tips for Instructional Services

The quality of each student's education depends on the effectiveness of teaching and learning. Reductions in funds could undermine the quality of instruction unless districts take the time to critically examine the issues at stake and establish priorities for decision making.

Some people consider budget reduction to involve cutting staff, stabilizing salaries, and increasing class size, but the key is actually finding the best ways available to improve the *effectiveness* of curriculum and instruction for the least amount of dollars. Ideas to consider are described in these pages.

### CURRICULUM OFFERINGS

- Conduct curriculum and course reviews to determine what can be eliminated, ranking programs by priority.
- Examine subject matter and methods to determine the feasibility of combining multiple courses into a single class period; e.g., second-, third-, and fourth-year foreign language together; pooled business education courses; pooled science and vocational courses. For example, you could institute a lab/cruise system in various science classes or vocational classes, where 15–22 kids or so in one class could do a va-

riety of different courses simultaneously. Such labs could be organized on an independent study basis with a tutor always present.
- Offer classes on alternating years such as chemistry one year and physics the next.
- Charge fees for student participation in nonrequired classes.

## Organization

- Eliminate kindergartens and provide structured activities for use in the home.
- Several districts, jointly or with a community college, could operate the more expensive educational programs or an alternative school.
- Approve early graduation for employed students and those ready for college-level work.
- Provide other options for reluctant attendees; reentry with dignity into the school program should remain as a feasible option.
- Allow more alternatives for credit: outside learning activities (private lessons or activities in music, athletics, art, or drama; work experience), credit by examination, open entry/open exit courses, home-study programs (correspondence, computer, Internet, and television), and performance-based programs.
- Allow students to challenge courses for credit by testing out of the course or demonstrating competency.

As caring respondents to the needs of our students, schools have taken on more and more responsibilities. Perhaps the time has come to push back just a bit by offering our facilities and access to the agencies and programs that genuinely ought to be fulfilling other needs and absolve ourselves of the responsibilities for actually providing them. For example, we could provide an in-school, integrated social services clinic but make it accessible to the County Health Department, Juvenile, Mental Health, Department of Human Resources, and similar programs. There are probably many other examples of agencies that could and should be coming to us to provide the service rather than expecting us to do it. Mental health services are just one example.

## INSTRUCTIONAL SERVICES

### Use of Time

- Consider the optimum number of days needed to accomplish curriculum goals.
- Consider year-round school.
- Combine instruction in related subjects.
- Establish a common staff preparation time prior to the arrival of students or after they leave.
- Increase academic learning time to help raise student achievement levels. (See, for example, Berliner 1983; Brophy 1979; Hawley, Rosenholtz, et al. 1984; Stallings 1980; and Walberg 1984.)
- Make the primary-age students' day longer to coordinate with the bus schedule, or consider a full day of instruction every other day.

### Staffing

- Analyze staff tasks to determine the most efficient ways to utilize employees and others (teachers, aides, volunteers, students, custodial, administrators, retired personnel, parents). Involve staff in suggesting ideas on cutting costs through such means as variable staffing patterns, flexible working hours, use of funds for substitutes, and so forth.
- Volunteers might serve as monitors of halls, buses, and playgrounds in place of paid personnel, club and organization advisors, and aides. Reward service with golden age cards, free lunches, or some other type of special recognition.
- Utilize parents and other volunteers to assist with in-school kindergarten or preschool activities.
- Identify instructional programs in which students can receive instruction while performing a service for the school/district. For example, students in word-processing classes could produce school correspondence and bulletins.
- Combine all levels of a particular sport for coaching and instruction.
- Increase the teacher-pupil ratio for lecture classes.

- Utilize cross-grade groupings.
- Eighth-grade students could be moved into the high school to better utilize staff and space. (Perhaps the eighth-graders' schedule could be different from the high school schedule.)

## Space and Equipment

- Provide teachers with work space, thus freeing classrooms for instructional purposes.
- Lease out any unused facilities or equipment.
- Where a facility or expertise is not available or would be unnecessarily duplicated, contract with the community (local offices, shops, hospitals, community college) to provide specialized instruction.
- Consider leasing or the lease option to purchase of equipment, rather than outright purchase. Explore the possibility of equipment grants from businesses within the area.
- Cooperatively purchase equipment used for short periods of time, rotating its use.
- Review the use of telephones to determine their need. A central telephone may be adequate for most purposes.

## Scheduling

- Consider year-round school operation.
- To conserve energy and expense, schedule school activities (e.g., athletics, music, and drama) during school hours, in the afternoon, or on Saturdays, instead of evenings.

## Materials

- Purchase only instructional materials that relate to specific instructional goals.
- Provide incentives for teachers to become more cost conscious in the use of instructional materials.
- Establish a regional clearinghouse to coordinate distribution of used and surplus textbooks, and to fill shortages.

- Consider using other relevant materials and the Internet to limit the number of textbooks needed.
- Consider using self-instructional materials for individualized programs (computer-assisted instruction, instructional learning systems, videotape, learning packages).
- Use outside resources to supplement school materials (local and state libraries; school library information systems providing online access to electronic media in the form of newspapers, periodicals, and so on; museums; businesses; and ESD materials centers).

## VOCATIONAL EDUCATION

### School Management

- Utilize the publication *Planning for Progress, Evaluating, and Planning for Vocational Education in Oregon* to review an existing, alternative, or new vocational program in terms of cost effectiveness.
- Use computers already in the school to help counselors with individual scheduling and program planning.
- Utilize the online Career Information System (CIS) for individualized vocational counseling.

### Staffing

- Manufacturing technology (industrial arts) and vocational agriculture classes could be combined, eliminating the need for one teacher.
- Reduce the duration of the vocational agriculture teacher's contract, from 240 days to 215, which still would allow for summer student project supervision and teacher in-service programs.

### Alternative Program Design

- Offer an open lab, with a teacher and an aide available to assist students; e.g., individualized accounting and secretarial classes, welding, and so forth.
- Where the vocational needs of students cannot be met at school, contract with business interests to teach classes in offices, shops, or hos-

pitals in the community. Develop cooperative programs with the local community college.

- Avoid duplication of programs in adjacent school districts and in multiple high school districts; share programs, equipment, and facilities.
- Emphasize such programs as job shadowing, cooperative work experience, internships, and apprenticeships to minimize the need for facilities and expensive equipment.

## Self-supporting Programs

- Include a unit on food preparation and catering in the home economics, food service cluster, or restaurant/tourism program that caters for actual events in school and outside, which could pay for the food used in training.
- Offer a manufacturing class, including the sale of student-manufactured goods. In this regard, all vocational programs should investigate profit possibilities in entrepreneurial program activities. Student-run businesses that generate a profit offsetting part or all of the cost of the course should be implemented, taking care not to compete with other businesses in your local community.
- Implement business incubators where students study how to start a small business, develop a business plan, and so forth for the first semester, and then choose one of the plans and put it into operation the second semester using the profits from the business to pay for the cost of the program and to leave seed money for the next year's class. *Case Study Example: Perrydale School District No. 21, Perrydale, Oregon:* For example, this author (Tim Adsit) served as superintendent/principal in one school from 1991–1997, where the FFA teacher started a T-shirt advertising business wherein students sold shirts with an outline of the county on them and sold businesses ads on the shirts in the approximate location where their business was located. The shirts were purchased for three dollars per shirt at wholesale and were sold at retail for fifteen dollars a shirt, while the ads sold for twenty dollars each. Net profits after one year were over $6,000. Entrepreneurial activities such as these teach students a marketable skill, namely, how to start your own small business. Some of the profits

were also used to offset the costs of the program so general school fund dollars did not have to be used to run the program. In addition, the other business plans developed by the students can be catalogued and placed on file in the school library for members of the general public wishing to review them and start a new local business. Many districts also have students continue the business after the end of the school year as a summer job or a way to earn money for college.

- Utilize student initiative and leadership through student leadership organizations to earn money for needed equipment and supplies.

## Equipment and Supplies

- Utilize computers for word processing.
- Solicit equipment contributions to school programs from local industry, state government, and so on.
- Acquire scrap materials from business and industry for classroom use, after which it can be returned to industry again to be sold as scrap.
- Make children's and infants' clothing in home economics or clothing construction classes; fewer supplies are required.
- Require that students pay a nonrefundable lost/broken tool fee.

## Advisory Committees

- Coordinate programs in such a way that an "umbrella-type" advisory committee could meet advisory committee requirements for high school, community college, and apprenticeship programs; ensure that membership is broad enough to accomplish the results desired.

## SPECIAL EDUCATION

Individualized instruction is essential to the student who is disabled; such instruction emphasizes each student's interests, abilities, motivation, goals, learning rate, and prognosis for moving ahead in the curriculum. Further, according to federal and state law, public schools are required to provide an appropriate education in the least restrictive environment to these students.

To meet the needs of this special population, districts need to develop approaches for handling reductions in funds and staff and still deliver services and meet maintenance of effort requirements. Districts might try the following ideas.

## Limitations on Services

- Use of stricter eligibility criteria would limit the number of handicapped students served. Those who are classified as "marginally" handicapped could be served through the regular school program.
- Diagnostic evaluations could be limited to the minimum required by law. Not all evaluation techniques and materials currently in use are essential, such as the practice of administering an IQ test to every student who might have a learning disability. Some practices could be eliminated without adversely affecting students.
- Surveying the tests in use in district and schoolwide special education programs, and limiting tests used to a few standardized tests mutually agreed upon to save expenses.

## Staffing

- Special education teachers, serving as consultants to regular classroom teachers, could help develop and manage handicapped students' IEPs, and oversee the delivery of services using a "consultive model."
- Hire teachers with special education certification as well as regular certification to teach in the regular class setting and provide special education services at the same time.
- Expand the use of paraprofessionals; e.g., instead of employing two teachers, employ one teacher and two aides.
- Encourage high school and college students, parents, and other volunteers in the district to serve as aides or teaching assistants.
- A special education teacher could handle more than one assignment; for example, a speech teacher also could serve as a speech/behavioral specialist.

- When there are only a few students with a particular handicapping condition, these students could be served in other classes for handicapped students, using aides as necessary.
- Join with other districts to deliver such services as physical therapy and occupational therapy.
- Seek help from community groups; for example, service clubs can plan special projects to generate funds and provide other assistance.
- When facing cutbacks in special education, it may be helpful to consider the following questions:

Current practice:

- Does an existing situation require a change?
- Are there only one to four students in one age group (elementary, junior high, high school) who need a program?
- Have the funding sources decreased so that it is no longer feasible to have a few students in a categorical, self-contained class?

Cost:

- What is the current cost of operation?
- What would the cost be with a new model?
- What is the most economical way to group students?

Personnel:

- Can programs be eliminated rather than personnel?
- Can personnel be used in other ways (e.g., as consultants rather than teachers)?
- Can current staff be used in a transdisciplinary approach?
- Is in-service training available for new staff roles in new models?

Building utilization:

- Will as many school facilities be needed?

Transportation:

- Are students being transported in the most economical way possible?
- Are students receiving services as close to home as possible? What are the placement options?
- How do students move from one program to another in the district?
- Will new eligibility data need to be gathered for new models?
- Are models being developed that address the needs of the low-incidence students?
- Can new models be developed without disturbing federal and state categorical funding channels?

Parents:

- Will parents be involved in creating new models?
- What will the extent of parent involvement be? What other options are there?
- Is a new model being developed that is functional?
- Have the needs of the students and resources available been assessed, and how do these two factors compare or differ?
- Have all options for models been explored?
- Have any ideas been excluded?
- Have the ideas allowed for openness and creativity?

## GUIDANCE PROGRAMS

When school districts take steps to cut costs, there is often a greater need for guidance services. The incidence of crime, suicide, and child abuse rises with the increase in the unemployment rate, thus creating many educational problems for the school. Increased stress on the family, coupled with limitations in class selections, curtailment of student activities and alternatives, and increased class size may be accompanied by more discipline and attendance problems, and increases in dropout rates.

Providing quality programs in a time of limited resources forces hard decisions: Should whole programs be cut? The school year be shortened?

Supplies cut in half? Professional development curtailed? These are just a few of the questions that educators are facing.

## Two Guiding Principles

Those who already have had to grapple with the dilemma of shrinking resources have found that:

- Program quality is preserved best by utilizing the most effective techniques available for delivery of instruction and services. With guidance, this means using classroom and group guidance techniques, teacher advisor programs, and trained volunteers, as well as the judicious use of paraprofessionals and the development of programs based on identified needs.
- Curtailing each program somewhat may be better than eliminating one or more programs altogether. However, when a program is significantly reduced in staff, the focus of the program also must be narrowed to maintain quality.

The cost-saving ideas below suggest ways to limit programs without permanently crippling services to students.

1. Assign counselors, administrators, and other support personnel as "duty substitutes" for one day per week.
2. Assign one period of teaching per day to six nonteaching staff members, saving the cost of one full-time employee (FTE) teaching position.
3. Using the "critical time" principle, save the funds spent on extended contracts for counselors, administrators, librarians, and other nonteaching staff members. Place counselors on contract for the same length of time as teachers, but readjust the scheduled work days for each counselor. For instance, since counselors need to be on duty the week before and the week after school opens, they could take two weeks off while school is in session. For most jobs, there are times when it is essential to accomplish certain tasks, and there are slack times. A counselor's slack time tends to occur the week prior to Christmas vacation, and in the middle of the third grading period.

The same applies for elementary principals: the two weeks prior to opening of school are far more critical than the weeks of Christmas and spring vacation.

4. Careful analysis of the work performed by an individual may show that someone else could assume some of the duties. Assign counselors to tasks in other areas where there have been staff reductions; at the same time, assign certain counselor tasks to others whose services cost less, including scheduling (to the teacher), educational advising (teacher), record-keeping (clerical staff), or routine schedule changes (secretarial staff).

5. Save one-third FTE by utilizing an intern counselor, teacher, administrator, or similar personnel when a vacancy occurs.

6. While it is not cost effective over the long run, the district could temporarily discontinue paying for staff travel, in-service training, attendance at conferences, supplementary materials, and college tuition. Counselors and others could be encouraged to assume these costs, claiming them as tax deductions. Cuts such as these may require bargaining in some states depending on your collective bargaining laws.

7. Save FTE by having counselors teach guidance-related classes, such as career education, career awareness, etc.


## MEDIA SERVICES

A school's media services support all instructional programs, and any reductions in school staff could result in larger class loads, which may lead to the need for more media support services. If the media program expenditures must be reduced, a task force representing the entire staff (e.g., administrators, media specialists, teachers, lay personnel) should be involved in making decisions about reductions.

In addition, school districts should be made more aware of the services available from the Department of Education in the area of media, which include instructional television, library services, audiovisual services, computers, distance education, and links to the state library system, local regional, national, and international databases via the Internet. Some cost-saving ideas are mentioned below:

## Administration

1. Give the district media coordinator (a position required by the Oregon State Standards for Public Schools, for example) more responsibility to coordinate and implement cost-saving ideas within the district media program to eliminate unnecessary duplication and procedures.
2. Consider the advantages and disadvantages of centralizing selected activities at the district level: purchase of materials, textbooks, and workbooks, printing services, the production of materials, and cataloging.
3. Consider the pros and cons of unifying the school and public libraries. Such an arrangement has been successful in certain communities.
4. When implementing federal and state program requirements to establish resource centers for Title I or similar programs, consider integration with existing media center facilities and management systems.
5. Schools should contact ESDs and other agencies for coordinating cost-saving services and information.
6. Consider a central depository for rarely used materials. Such cooperation may be feasible within a district, between several districts, or through an ESD.
7. Be sure a materials selection policy is developed and implemented for the district.
8. Eliminate cataloging at the building level; currently, much time is wasted on recataloging preprocessed materials.
9. Consider installing an electronic security system in the media center. Studies have shown that such systems have paid for themselves within two and one-half years.
10. Consider the pros and cons of computerizing and automating the card catalog.
11. Keep current on developments in instructional technology for media programs and instruction (e.g., computers in schools).
12. Conduct a flea market or auction and sell items (books, authorized equipment, small furniture, and so forth) that are no longer needed or used by the school. Proceeds may be used to meet a specific media program need; increased space may be another benefit. Be sure

to follow your state laws and district policies on getting rid of surplus equipment.

13. Consider the pros and cons of collecting fees on lost, damaged, or stolen books, or require students to perform work to repay costs incurred.

14. Seek out donations for materials and funds from public and private sources. Any materials donated should meet district specifications.

## Services

15. When applicable, obtain copyright release to reprint only those portions of textbooks and supplementary materials that are used in the district's instructional program.

16. Consider the cost effectiveness of photocopying as opposed to offset printing.

17. If you have not already done so, consider the use of videocassettes, CDs, and DVDs in place of 16mm format.

18. Encourage teachers to utilize in-school television programming, provided at no charge by several national programs such as Cable in the Classroom, or those programs broadcast by your particular state's Public Broadcasting Service.

19. Consider the use of computers in the media centers for library management applications, as well as for instructional and research purposes.

## Materials

20. Arrange for increased resource sharing among schools, districts, ESDs, and such other agencies as public libraries, community colleges, or special libraries.

21. Consider cooperative purchasing of materials and periodicals within districts, between districts, through ESDs, or through regional organizations. A single bidding process still allows for independent purchases by cooperating schools and districts. Product quality and cost saving can be assured in the written contract, and bigger bid packages will yield greater discounts.

22. Evaluate frequency of use of periodicals; prioritize them according to use and need; discontinue low-priority subscriptions.

23. When older books (library materials and textbooks) will continue to be used, consider rebinding rather than purchasing new copies.

24. Consider a temporary moratorium on the purchase of books for a given curriculum area. Subscriptions for periodicals and newspapers should be maintained.

25. Weed collections of old, outdated materials.

## Equipment

26. Purchase expensive equipment cooperatively.

27. Investigate the pros and cons of equipment maintenance contracts.

28. Consider the advantages and disadvantages of a lease option when purchasing equipment.

29. When cost effective, use shop classes or projects to build items for the media center/school.

30. Consolidate media equipment repair for several districts.

31. Refinish furniture or equipment rather than making new purchases.

32. When cost effective, store equipment and materials from schools that are temporarily closed. A careful inventory should be maintained.

## COST-SAVING IDEAS

### Curriculum: Expanded Idea #1

High schools offer specialized science courses to relatively small numbers of students, making science instruction an area of high cost. A well-coordinated science program can be developed that will reduce costs while providing a complete high school science curriculum.

*Advantages:* Class size may be increased, particularly in smaller districts—science instruction may be more effective; allows for greater staff flexibility.

*Disadvantages:* Science staff members lose their unique identities—the public does not see clearly labeled science courses; students do not necessarily understand that they have taken an equivalent to a given specialty.

*Additional Information:* At least one FTE science staff might be saved in a high school of 600 students. Initially, a sum of money may need to be set aside for such factors as larger class enrollment, introducing new content, special exercises, and integrating the subject areas. Students could learn how to apply scientific knowledge and skills in an integrated way to solve everyday problems.

## Instruction: Expanded Idea #2

Many of the tasks currently assigned to administrators, when broken down into small jobs, can be carried out by paraprofessionals following short-term training. This requires precise analysis of job descriptions, so that responsibilities can be itemized.

*Advantages:* Administrative costs can be reduced; the time spent on the task can be increased; such task analysis might be applied to other programs.

*Disadvantages:* Less status may be assigned to a task; less attention may be paid to the exact interpretation of laws and regulations; more than one person becomes responsible for a program or program component.

*Additional Information:* There will be concern over job losses due to replacement by paraprofessionals. The adoption of this concept could save significantly on administrator time, which could be diverted to direct instruction or supervision of instructional programs. The principal might be responsible for greater instructional leadership in specialized areas.

## Instruction: Expanded Idea #3

It has been found that if the amount of time spent directly on learning a task can be increased, there is a significant chance that student achievement levels can be increased. The best method of increasing learning time is to improve classroom management and provide direct instruction. This currently is being done in many districts and programs in use across the country.

*Advantages:* Greater achievement for the dollar invested in teacher time; student attitudes improve toward school; improved student assessment program.

*Disadvantages:* There is estimated to be an initial cost of $200 for startup materials per classroom; increased regimentation of learning.

*Additional Information:* The initial cost of entering the program and maintenance of student progress records probably will increase material costs, but there may be fewer expenses for behavioral concerns. Students can assume more responsibility for their own behavior, and teachers analyze their actions more carefully.

## Instruction: Expanded Idea #4

*Case Study Example: Northwest Textbook Depository, Portland, Oregon:* A clearinghouse system can be established for textbooks that are available, in surplus, or for which there is a shortage.

*Advantages:* Allows districts to reduce the inventory of current texts that they must carry; spares and replacements will be easier to locate; bid prices are frozen for a minimum of two years, which saves the district money on the purchase of new textbooks bought in quantity during the implementation period; useful life of text series will be extended by making replacements easier; better utilization will be made of inventories around the state; existing texts can be re-adopted more easily, rather than having to adopt new series due to unavailability of texts.

*Disadvantages:* Requires labor and materials to establish and maintain a central file of needs and preferences; materials could be entered into computer file by ISBN for faster, easier match-ups.

*Additional Information:* It is not known what the supply of surplus books is at this time, or how that compares with district needs around the state, but a simple inventory could be conducted by your respective state departments of education or some other agreed-upon agency.

## Vocational Education: Expanded Idea #5

Limit the specialized vocational education program to the junior/senior level, and teach only those occupational skills that are considered vital for entering the labor market using studies such as the *SCANS* report to identify vital occupational skills. Most high schools are now geared toward introductory programs; ninth- and tenth-graders would take introductory courses designed to give them a sense of things to come.

*Advantages:* Requires school districts to hire teachers who are specialists in their fields; makes possible the use of specialists who teach the same occupational skill in more than one vocational area.

*Disadvantages:* Small school districts would not be able to do this because they do not have enough students.

## Vocational Education: Expanded Idea #6

Two or more school districts could offer a joint program, available to all students.

*Advantages:* Districts jointly finance the costs, assisted by state and federal vocational funds to pay for the cost overage; could lead to full enrollments and the provision of more adequate equipment; surplus U.S. government equipment frequently is available, which can be obtained if adequate use can be shown; joint use of facilities would also require use of instructors in common, but this will not necessarily create difficulties.

## Special Education: Expanded Idea #7

*Case Study Example:* Combine two classes, each with a teacher and an aide, into one class with one teacher and two aides. For example, to cut costs, a class of ten students with severe language learning difficulties was combined with a class of fifteen with severe learning disabilities. Both classes had been self-contained. The combined class was assigned to a teacher and two aides. Additional support was added to the program by increasing the amount of time the speech and language pathologist worked with students. In addition, another special education teacher provided some training in language development.

*Advantages:* The district was able to eliminate the need for one teacher, who accepted a regular classroom teaching position.

*Disadvantages:* It was more difficult to meet the educational needs of the students, even though the teacher in this case was considered particularly able. The teacher must be able to function as a planner/supervisor, with aides handling a considerable amount of the actual instruction; one parent felt that the larger class size resulted in less-than-adequate instruction, and the district was involved in a due process hearing (the district won the hearing).

*Additional Information:* The district contracted with one less teacher—a savings of approximately $45,000. The due process hearing cost the district approximately $6,000, plus the staff time involved. To a much greater degree, the teacher must be able to assume the role of a classroom manager and be able to deliver services through aides. Additional support services may be needed. Since implementing the change, special education enrollment has increased in one class to the point where the teacher assigned language development responsibilities could no longer assist the class. At the same time, another district special education class dropped in enrollment; students in this class were transferred to two other similar classes. Their teacher then took half of the children from the combined class. The final result was the two original classes with one teacher and one aide each, and one less class.

## Special Education: Expanded Idea #8

Combine severely and moderately handicapped students in a classroom with one teacher and one aide. Normally there would be a teacher for the moderately handicapped and one teacher for the severely handicapped. The latter group would be served with aides through what is known as the "rural model."

*Advantages:* The moderately handicapped students serve as models for the more severely handicapped. The model saves costs of providing "rural model" services that would require the services of one full-time aide for each severely handicapped student; transportation can be combined for severe and moderate students, and some can ride regular buses.

*Disadvantages:* The model requires a teacher who can and will serve both severely and moderately handicapped in a single setting. Students are viewed as belonging to a special class and regular teachers are reluctant to have these students in their classes, as opposed to a situation where students who are based in a homeroom go to a resource room.

*Additional Information:* The first year the teacher had to conduct public relations information work with the school; the model is based on a small population of handicapped students. The special education students performed well; the program is effective and is well accepted in the school (K–3).

## Special Education: Expanded Idea #9

Districts may be able to cut costs by contracting for specific instructional services that, in the past, have been provided by staff personnel. One district has contracted for physical therapy and occupational therapy, and plans to contract for home instruction. In addition, the district is considering contracting for services to be provided to low-incident students, such as the severely emotionally disturbed. Contracting out makes particular sense because of the rising costs of benefits.

*Advantages:* Services can be contracted at a fixed rate for a fixed duration of time. The one district's rate is equal to the district's contracted summer rate—the amount that teachers are paid for summer work beyond their regular contract ($22.00 per hour). Regular district pay averages over $237 per day, considerably above the contractual rate.

The district does not have to pay fixed costs on contracts, which normally fall between 38 and 42 percent of salary costs. If the contractor is not meeting the performance standards of the contract, the contract can be terminated. At present, there are no job losses, as contracting is utilized only when natural attrition occurs.

*Disadvantages:* Staff personnel who performed the services in the past must be reassigned; until now, attrition has solved this problem for the one district. Programs must be supervised and evaluated by district staff to maintain quality services. It takes time to locate qualified staff and turnover may be greater. Using this method implies school staffing for IEP development, supervision of the services, and the availability of qualified contractors, as well as the utilization of the resources of larger metropolitan areas, ESDs, or district cooperatives.

*Additional Information:* There should be little impact on students.

## Student Services: Expanded Idea #10

Utilize support personnel as substitute teachers. Assign counselors, administrators, and other support personnel for "duty substitute" one day per week (e.g., if a substitute is needed Monday, one counselor serves while other counselors remain on assignment; if a substitute is needed Tuesday, another counselor serves, and so on). Other nonteaching staff would serve in the same way.

*Advantages:* The district would be able to save the cost of one FTE substitute salary for every five persons involved in this process. Utilizing support personnel in this manner will preserve 80 percent of the services of those involved in the "duty substitute program."

*Disadvantages:* The "duty substitute program" will reduce the services available to students, teachers, and parents by 20 percent (i.e., each counselor will function as a counselor only four days per week).

*Additional Information:* The district coordinator can develop the specific scheduling procedures in cooperation with building principals and support personnel prior to implementation. The concept should be explained to all staff members as procedures are developed.

## Student Services: Expanded Idea #11

*Case Study Example: Crane Union High School, Crane, Oregon:* Have guidance staff teach related courses. In the past fifteen years, a number of districts in Oregon, for example, have maintained a moderately staffed guidance program by utilizing counselors to teach courses. Because counselors are required to hold teacher certification and have teaching experience prior to receiving counselor certification, each counselor in the state is proficient in one or more subject areas. (Counselors coming into Oregon from other states may lack teaching experience.) While some districts have utilized counselors to teach one or two periods per day in their primary teaching field, most now use them to teach related courses such as career education, psychology, leadership skills, or communication skills.

*Advantages:* One FTE staff can be saved if there are enough counselors or personnel available to combine counselor duties with other staff functions to fill one teaching slot. In large schools, each of the two counselors might teach one period and the activities director, librarian, vice principal, or a central office staff person might do the same. This maintains a basic program but at a reduced level.

*Disadvantages:* Based on a six-period day, 17 percent is lost of each counseling position's time if the counselor teaches one class. This means a reduction in the results that can be expected in the counseling program. It also means less flexibility for the individuals involved. Parents, away-from-school activities, and emergencies take second place when class is in session.

*Additional Information:* Since counselors, librarians, and administrators all have advanced training, this approach may mean that the district is paying slightly more for each class taught than for the same class taught by regular teachers. Eighty-three percent of each program may be preserved. This approach requires that the staff involved maintain expertise in two fields, which adds to the demands placed on them.

## Student Services: Expanded Idea #12

Utilize a paraprofessional to perform many duties that do not require professional expertise. For example, in a school of two FTE counselors, assign 1.5 FTE counselors and .5 FTE paraprofessional. The paraprofessional assumes scheduling, record keeping, attendance checking, or other duties assigned to the counselor.

*Advantages:* Yields a cost savings of approximately 50 percent of a professional's salary by utilizing a paraprofessional. Paraprofessionals are often more efficient at some of these duties. Supplies students with an additional contact; not all counselors relate to all students.

*Disadvantages:* Reduces assigned counseling time available to students.

*Additional Information:* The paraprofessional needs training in handling of confidential information, record keeping, telephone, and similar duties.

## Student Services: Expanded Idea #13

*Case Study Example: Corbett School District, Corbett, Oregon:* Utilize teachers to provide guidance services (e.g., "Guide Program—Assign guidance responsibilities to be shared among teaching staff).

*Advantages:* Reduces the number of assigned counselors; teachers become closer and more familiar with students; teachers become more aware of the total school program.

*Disadvantages:* Could result in taking teaching time away from the classroom; some teachers are not well prepared to accept guidance and counseling responsibilities; teachers may resist the assignment.

*Additional Information:* Clear and specific task assignments need to be made.

An in-service program may be needed to prepare administrators, counselors, and teachers to implement the program. Care should be taken in matching teachers and students. The program must be monitored and evaluated, with feedback to teachers on the effectiveness of the program.

## Student Services: Expanded Idea #14

Use a "Mobile Guidance Unit" to provide guidance and counseling services to small rural school districts or schools within a district.

*Advantages:* Professional guidance and counseling services would be available and costs shared by several districts or schools; shared facilities and equipment would reduce costs to any single district; the counselor is utilized as a resource person to teaching staff.

*Disadvantages:* The counselor is not a member of the school staff; the counselor is not available for crisis counseling; time is needed to coordinate activities and for travel; longer working days for the counselor sometimes result; there is an initial cost for materials and the mobile unit.

*Additional Information:* Requires coordination and cooperative agreements among several districts; requires a counselor who can establish good working relationships with many schools and districts; requires a steering committee to evaluate the program and make recommendations on improvement.

## Student Services: Expanded Idea #15

Analyze procedures for assisting some students to make a successful transition to alternative education programs. Assist these students to seek education or work through private programs supported by flow-through from basic school support funds or jobs in business and industry.

*Advantages:* Reduces youth unemployment through successful transition from school to work; attendance rates improve; achievement test scores rise among youth who find meaning in their education programs; intervention at an early age has greater promise of productive lifetime employment.

*Disadvantages:* Communities may feel the effects of youths' presence in the community, with a possible increase in juvenile court referrals and crime; some communities may view the alternative program as a failure for the student or the school; basic school support funds would not be received if students are not enrolled in school or alternative programs.

*Additional Information:* Greater sensitivity to the needs of students and knowledge of the law specific to alternative programs will be necessary to make this process effective. Adequate criteria for identification and placement of students need to be developed. Care should be exercised to involve parents whenever possible in any decision related to the education of students.

## Student Services: Expanded Idea #16

Have counselors work with the emotionally handicapped. Utilize one or more counselors to work part time with emotionally handicapped students in a classroom. These students could carry as much of the regular program as possible, while attending this class one or two periods daily.

*Advantages:* Assists in mainstreaming students who have emotional handicaps, while producing a cost savings due to the fact that the district does not need to employ a special education teacher for this group of students.

*Disadvantages:* Reduces counseling time available to all students. Places additional responsibilities on some counselors; not all counselors can work effectively with the emotionally handicapped.

*Additional Information:* The cost of hiring a half-time teacher for emotionally handicapped is about $22,500. This cost could be saved by involving two or more counselors. The cost saving would be proportionate to the number of students served.

Students would be assisted in adapting to the school environment. Some counselors might require additional training.

## Media Services: Expanded Idea #17

The district media coordinator could be given the authority to handle the ordering and use of expensive items on a districtwide basis; in some cases, this may involve close coordination with building administrators. Coordinating the purchase and use at the district level can reduce costs and avoid duplication.

*Advantages:* Could eliminate some duplication of items; coordinates sharing of items between schools (e.g., VCRs and computers) not in constant use; allows for the coordinated purchase of expensive hardware; establishes a clearinghouse for locating items.

*Disadvantages:* In addition to the building principal, another individual will be involved in media purchases; some inconveniences in time for purchasing may occur; some inconvenience may result because of shared use of items; sharing of items may mean reduced services until the fiscal situation improves. Fiscal savings amounts will vary depending on current efficiency of school district coordination.

## Media Services: Expanded Idea #18

Periodicals are purchased by all schools, and community colleges; they are the best source of current information available. It may be possible to obtain additional discounts from subscription service agencies through cooperative purchasing arrangements or to purchase subscription services online such as EBSCO*host* Electronic Journals Service (EJS) (http://ejournals.ebsco.com). Such arrangements may be within districts, between districts, through ESDs, or through regional organizations.

*Advantages:* Additional discounts may be possible; periodical ordering by participating libraries can be better controlled; better cooperation in ordering and sharing of low-use, high-cost periodicals; may encourage more cooperation among libraries.

*Disadvantages:* Copying and copyright problems may occur; close cooperation and coordination in initial stages will be required; problems in obtaining periodicals may occur at individual libraries; time frame for settling problems may be extended.

*Additional Information:* More cooperation on the part of libraries would probably occur. Unified lists of serials (periodicals) for the participating libraries would allow for better knowledge of access to periodicals in a given area. Students and teachers would have access to a wider array of material to support instructional programs.

## Media Services: Expanded Idea #19

Consider rebinding old and damaged textbooks, as well as other instructional materials, rather than replacing them with new copies.

*Advantages:* Cost of replacement through binding is roughly 35 to 40 per cent of new copy price (binding costs $8–$10 per volume; new, $20–$22); extends the usable life of text and library materials.

*Disadvantages:* Coordination is needed; materials are not available while in binding; criteria for binding need to be developed.

*Additional Information:* Good staff coordination is required; good communication with the bindery is needed. Criteria for rebinding need to be developed.

## Media Services: Expanded Idea #20

Install electronic security systems in media centers.

*Advantages:* Reduces the loss of books and other materials from media centers; results in sizable financial savings to the district; increases the availability and quantity of learning materials; reduces the "police role" of the library staff, allowing more time for direct service.

*Disadvantages:* The initial cost of installation would increase the budget; school districts that have installed such systems have recouped initial costs within one or two years, with substantial savings over longer periods of time.

## Media Services: Expanded Idea #21

Consider unifying the school and public libraries; it has worked well for certain communities.

*Advantages:* Allows for common utilization of one library facility; allows for common utilization of a larger collection of materials; combines selection and purchase of materials for potential discount; allows for facility use during the day, as well as during evening hours and on weekends; allows the public more exposure to the school setting.

*Disadvantages:* Adults may not feel comfortable sharing a facility and materials with students; adult materials may need to be segregated; may require more staffing by professionals and nonprofessionals; will require combining of the card catalogs of public and school libraries.

*Additional Information:* Representatives from both the school and community need to be involved. Local laws and statutes need to be consulted. Communication with the public is critical throughout the process.

## Media Services: Expanded Idea #22

Out-of-date or seldom-used materials should be removed selectively from the media center and classrooms. Such removal allows for additional shelf space and more efficient use of the media center. Many regional service districts (Boards of Cooperative Educational Services (BOCES) and ESDs) are eliminating their media centers because of the rising costs for circulation. If you were to ask just how much it costs to circulate a book in the county where you live, if you have a regional library, the costs would be stunning. There are many new alternatives such as online services, electronic books accessed via the Internet, and so forth.

*Advantages:* More shelf space, more up-to-date collection of materials; better utilization of existing equipment; more efficient housekeeping; elimination of materials that are irrelevant to the curriculum.

*Disadvantages:* Material removed may be needed at some later date; takes time and staff to develop criteria for removal.

*Additional Information:* Good criteria needs to be developed for the removal of materials and equipment, and competent staff need to be assigned responsibility for removal.

## Media Services: Expanded Idea #23

The district should develop a districtwide materials selection policy to ensure that only relevant materials are purchased to support the curriculum and leisure reading needs of students and teachers.

*Advantages:* Costly random purchasing of materials may be eliminated; improves quality of materials; may encourage more cooperation in selection and purchase of materials; criteria for selection may eliminate censorship problems.

*Disadvantages:* Takes time to develop a sound policy.

*Additional Information:* Good selection criteria need to be developed; leadership in information needed to manage the selection process. The state department of education may have guidelines for developing a selection policy.

## Media Services: Expanded Idea #24

*Case Study Example: Crane Union High School District 1J, Crane, Oregon:* Teachers should be encouraged to utilize in-school television curriculum provided by the various satellite networks, Cable in the Classroom, V-Tel, or similar programs; in many states, the department of education either has its own network, or broadcasts via the state's Public Broadcasting Service.

*Advantages:* Each series is a designed curriculum sequence encompassing a full unit of study. The series may be provided at no fee by the department in some cases, or at fairly low cost by commercial service providers. Resources may include, in many states, an annual in-school program schedule provided by the department of education to each school at no charge. It describes each series and tells the dates, times of broadcast, and titles of each program within the series. Such distance-learning technologies ease the burden of the larger class sizes that teachers are facing and allow districts to expand the curriculum without expanding the staff. They also form a base of student knowledge from which teachers can build toward higher levels of learning. Low-cost teacher's guides are available for most series, which often include student exercises ($2–$6).

*Disadvantages:* At present, many schools across the nation cannot receive Public Broadcasting due to lack of infrastructure and equipment. A video recorder may be necessary if series are not broadcast at convenient times for your local school schedule. Supervisory staff, a "distance learning mentor," or a "contact teacher" may have to be assigned to supervise students even though they are working independently with a teacher over the particular mode of distance education being utilized.

## COST-EFFECTIVE INSTRUCTION CASE STUDY EXAMPLES

Schools were originally designed to bring together students in groups of twenty-five and provide each group with a teacher. At the elementary level, they generally spent almost the entire day with one teacher. At the secondary level, they moved to a new teacher each hour, but always in groups of approximately twenty-five. While many things have changed in public education, the use of this model is fairly consistent.

As demands for a broader and more complex curriculum have risen and as smaller schools have struggled to offer a comprehensive array of courses, the "twenty-five model" has been challenged. And, as schools have faced the mandates of serving a changing student clientele, the old model is difficult to perpetuate.

Since even the funding model is generally built around the notion of twenty-five students per teacher in one way or another, any diversion from the fundamental numbers helps create a financial challenge. To date, schools have only begun to look at alternatives. The search for other avenues of cost-effective instruction is often hampered by labor agreements that also are built around providing approximately one teacher for each twenty-five students and ensuring that the instruction is delivered by members of the bargaining unit. Most state and federal laws are also built upon much the same premise. Therefore, almost all aspects of the system are designed to perpetuate a resource allocation model and instructional design that may not be ideal for addressing changing needs.

This look at the issues surrounding the challenge of reducing instructional costs may be more of an identification of the problem rather than a treatise on solutions; however, several ideas in this regard have been included.

## Online Learning

Distance education or online learning is gradually making headway in small districts and large ones as well. Salem-Keizer, a district of 37,000 students, is one of Oregon's leaders in the design of online instruction. So, too, is the Southern Oregon ESD, which serves Medford, another of Oregon's largest, along with the ESD that serves Albany, yet another fairly large district. Medford and a number of other districts are served by Oregon On-Line, which was formerly Southern Oregon On-Line School (SOOS). Albany and others are served by COOL School, a product of the Linn/Benton/Lincoln ESD.

In the North Central ESD, students in a group of small, remote districts are served by the Frontier Learning Network, which is a combination of online classes shared between the districts and a project, which actually takes some instruction to the site through the use of portable classrooms that are transported from one community to another. The Frontier Learning Network is funded by a special grant from the Oregon legislature. The primary school districts served by the Frontier Learning Network are Sherman County, Arlington, Condon, Fossil, Mitchell, and Spray.

Although online learning is of critical value to small districts in terms of helping to level the playing field in terms of scope of offerings, the concept is of equal interest to large districts that are also looking at cost-effective methods of providing a broad array of course offerings.

One of the keys to the effective use of online learning is to install the capacity to help students easily access distance education opportunities and to provide the necessary support for their ongoing participation.

Districts moving into this area are confronting a number of challenges, such as training for online instructors, contract issues related to both teaching online and the use of distance education in lieu of regular class-room teachers, funding for the costs of online classes, funding for staff to help supervise access to distance education, and budget issues surrounding equipment and other materials to support this concept. With the growing use of technology in public education, it is a sure bet, however, that online learning will continue to grow at an exponential rate.

## The Learning Lab

As enrollment at the South Wasco County High School in Maupin, Oregon, has diminished, staff and administrators have continually been in search of ways to continue offering a broader curriculum in the midst of staff declines.

One answer to their efforts has been the creation of the "Learning Center," a popular program housed in a modern portable unit adjacent to the old secondary building. Staffed by a licensed teacher and an aide, the program hosts a steady stream of students with a wide variety of needs. This is where the talented and gifted are introduced to unique courses that their small high school cannot offer.

And this is where students behind in their credits are able to get back on track toward graduation. The Learning Center is also an important part of instruction for the school's growing ELL (English-language learner) population. With limited capacity to address the needs of second-language learners, the school has turned to the Learning Center to provide enhanced coursework as part of the transition process.

Students are generally limited to one class per day in the Learning Center, although some have been allowed to take two. The program can handle twenty or more students per period on an almost individualized basis.

South Wasco's Learning Center is not unlike the lab approach being used in other smaller high schools where small enrollments play havoc with scheduling. But it is a concept that could just as well find a home in larger high schools where declining resources have limited the scope of the curriculum.

In the lab approach, a teacher—in business education, for example—might not be able to offer separate classes in bookkeeping, typing, business English, and so forth. Instead, the teacher offers a laboratory approach where small groups of students take various courses during the same period. One group of three or four might be taking beginning bookkeeping while another group is taking advanced coursework in the same subject. Across the room, two students are enrolled in business English while three more are learning to type. This approach provides an opportunity for students to experience a broader curriculum even if there aren't enough to justify individual classes.

In some larger high schools, this same approach is being used for classes such as foreign languages. In French or even German, for example, where enrollments might be declining, the program can be kept intact through the use of the laboratory approach.

A modification is being used in Ione where calculus and precalculus are combined because the total enrollment in the two classes is about ten students.


## MEDIA SERVICES CASE STUDY EXAMPLE


A generation ago, most schools had librarians who presided over a collection of learning resources consisting primarily of books and encyclopedias. And education service districts were literally founded on the concept of distributing 16mm films and other resources that were too costly for individual schools to purchase. Films that once may have cost hundreds of dollars are now available on tape or disk for a fraction of that price.

In the wake of technological advancements, the 16mm film has become all but obsolete and many ESDs are going out of the media business. Through the use of the Internet, low-cost videotapes, CDs, DVDs, and a host of other new advancements, schools have almost immediate access to a whole new world of learning resources.

Library materials from around the world are available to students who simply log on to a computer in their classroom. As a result, as schools have come face-to-face with declining resources, the traditional library has undergone a dramatic change. In districts of 2,000 or more students, it is sometimes difficult to find even one certified library/media specialist. Often, they have been replaced by aides who are primarily assigned the task of checking books in and out.

This has resulted in a disconnection between the school's collection of learning resources and the classroom. In an effort to use the aide concept and yet enjoy some of the benefits of a certificated librarian, some schools are turning to a regional service agency, are using district-level personnel, or are contracting with outside professionals to provide them with the benefits that are to be gained from someone trained in the field.

The use of these professional personnel on a short-term basis assures that someone will be continually examining the collection and providing a balanced array of learning resources. There will also be a person who can meet with the staff and tie together the classroom with the school library. This person can also provide training for the library aide.

One such example is the Ione School District, which has budgeted for fifteen days per year of service by a licensed media specialist. As part of this fifteen-day contract, the individual will be expected to:

- Assist with professional development and training for the library aide
- Audit the library/media collection and recommend purchases
- Work with classroom teachers to help create a closer interface between the curriculum and available library resources
- Help provide in-service training to classroom teachers regarding the use of the district's library/media resources
- Recommend and help coordinate programs that stimulate reading

## SPECIAL EDUCATION: VIDEOCONFERENCING COST SAVINGS EXAMPLE

With medical costs rising, some districts, working cooperatively with regional agencies, have started bringing evaluation clinics to rural areas rather than trying to have families experience the high costs associated with spending a day or two in a metropolitan area.

By holding periodic, daylong clinics, they are able to assemble highly skilled professionals at a single location that is more accessible to families.

And rather than having medical specialists travel long distances and spend valuable time en route to and from a diagnosis, they are turning to video-conferencing as a way of helping bridge the distance gap. When it fits the situation, this tool is not only effective but it also allows professionals to interact at a much-reduced cost.

In the state of Oregon, and elsewhere, videoconferencing is being used more and more to conduct meetings that used to take considerable amounts of staff time, as well as expenses for mileage, plane fare, lodging, and other travel expenses. People from around the state can now meet for an hour or two without having to add six or eight hours of travel each way.

While telephone conferences have been used on occasion for a number of years, being able to actually view the speakers adds a new dimension. And sometimes, to retain the spirit of collegiality, groups will sometimes meet regionally to participate in such conferences.

## CASE STUDY EXAMPLE: SUMMER SCHOOL COST SAVINGS

A group of school districts in Umatilla and Morrow Counties, Oregon, have traditionally offered a migrant summer school. They have also tried offering a regular summer school program but were interested in finding a cost-effective way to serve both groups.

Several years ago, they combined the migrant summer school with the regular school district summer school program and contracted with the ESD to oversee all of the programs. As a result of combining the program, they experienced efficiencies with administrative oversight, facilities, in-structional materials, support staff, transportation, and meal services.

# 4

## Cost-saving Tips for Support Services

### BUILDINGS AND GROUNDS

#### Energy Conservation

Energy costs have increased astronomically over the past five years, and although the pace has abated somewhat at this time, it is predicted that costs again will increase significantly over the next five years. Effective use of all available energy sources needs to be reconsidered periodically in light of emerging technologies and concepts.

1. In this era of high fuel prices, a comprehensive energy conservation program for the district is an absolute necessity.
2. Periodically reemphasize ongoing energy conservation programs.
3. Ask the local power company to conduct an on-site energy audit of the school building.
4. Ask the mechanical engineer who originally designed equipment for the building to evaluate the effectiveness of heating controls. Large districts might train their maintenance staff to repair the controls for heating and ventilating systems.
5. Save heating costs significantly by starting school earlier in the year (e.g., in the middle of August) and extending Christmas vacation for two weeks before Christmas. Secondary students could seek temporary employment and school maintenance could be accomplished during that time.

6. Install heating and ventilating systems controlled by computer; such systems can help make better use of energy.
7. Improve heat energy sources through energy grants. Consider a change from diesel heating fuel to wood pellet, or similar changes, or consider the use of geothermal sources, if available, to heat your plant.
8. Now that solar technology has improved, installations are proving more cost effective than originally predicted. For example, swimming pool and shower water can be solar heated in Oregon from May through mid-October. In this regard, solar system suppliers are becoming more competitive and districts should research all possibilities.
9. Consolidate the use of space, such as closing wings or units of buildings to save on heating and ventilating costs.
10. Continue replacement of incandescent lighting with fluorescent in schools. Although short-term capital expenditures are necessary, fluorescent lighting will reduce costs in the long run.
11. Disconnect electrical appliances (e.g., refrigerators, freezers) during summer vacation.

## Use of Buildings

School buildings serve a function—to provide a learning environment— and when the building is not used for that function, it is not working at capacity. Encourage effective building use during the regularly scheduled school day, and all other hours as well.

1. Schedule building space and let groups know when space is available for community use. Have someone on duty one or two nights a week; do not simply leave the building open for use any time. In this way, better use is made of facilities when they are open.
2. Consider using the high school as a community center, since it is one of the most frequently used buildings in the community. Include a number of activities normally scheduled at the local elementary school. Any fee for using high school facilities could be lower than fees for junior high and elementary schools. This would encourage the community to use those buildings that are opened already and supervised by night custodial staff.

3. Adult education courses provided in school facilities could be charged the full fee, including utility expenditures. If adult education courses do not pick up this cost, then, in effect, the taxpaying community is subsidizing those who are taking courses. Good management dictates that such fees be charged.

4. Explore whether the use of facilities by special interest groups is appropriate. You may not want to be accused of subsidizing special interest groups should the district not have the resources to fully fund the basic education program.

5. Explore the joint use of facilities with other governmental agencies. Allow them to use spaces that are unoccupied at the present time, separating them from areas used by staff and students, and providing separate entrances to the building. Amortize the capital outlay required for remodeling over a five-year period. Share costs of building operations with other occupants.

## Maintenance of Buildings

Deferred building maintenance only postpones the inevitable expenditure of funds. For every maintenance dollar not spent now, probably one dollar and twenty cents' worth of maintenance will be needed a year from now. Keep exact records of maintenance that has been deferred and the impact on the instructional program.

1. Districts traditionally have emphasized the need for continuing professional growth of certificated staff through seminars, workshops, and additional academic credit. However, regular training for classified employees often is overlooked. Continuous employee training and periodic performance reviews are two important techniques for cost savings with custodial and light maintenance personnel. (See Business Task Force on Education, *Public School Survey and Recommendations* (March 1969): 47–56.)

2. Roof maintenance is a very technical matter and funds often are wasted on roofing programs that are not well conceived. Established criteria are needed for the selection of a roofer, particularly when working with built-up roofs. In cases where a roofer has done work for the district previously, determine the quality of that work and

always seek references with whom you can discuss quality of roofers' previous work.

3. Evaluate maintenance costs to determine whether repairs should be done by the staff or on contract; consider the cost effectiveness of replacement instead of repairs.
4. Contract maintenance and custodial programs.
5. Purchase products and use building designs in new construction that are designed to reduce vandalism.

## Cleaning of Buildings

The public expects education to be conducted in a safe and healthy environment, and "healthy" means clean and orderly. While this is an area where savings may be found, overall quality cannot be reduced.

1. A good relationship between custodial and other staff members can effectively cut costs. When classrooms are kept orderly, much less work is required of the custodian. Removal of chalk dust is appreciated by the teaching staff. The teachers should report to the custodian routine maintenance tasks that are needed, and the principal periodically should inspect the buildings with the custodian to see that standards are maintained.
2. A list of technical experts should be available so that district staff can obtain specialized help when it is needed.
3. Factors to consider when contracting for custodial services include cost, the size of the facility, facility construction, and the types of programs conducted in that facility. Thoroughly analyze the job responsibilities of current staff to determine where contracted services are warranted; carefully determine whether contracting would impede the flexibility of facility use or staff and student interrelationships with those providing custodial services. Security is yet another consideration. Note: custodial and maintenance services are not defined as "personal services" by the Public Contract Review Board. They must be bid out, and it is necessary to obtain certification of the "going wage rate" from the bidder.
4. Use staff development programs to prepare custodial employees to assume added responsibilities.

5. Any changes in the maintenance program or operating schedules need to be agreed upon by the building principal, the custodian, and the central office personnel responsible for the maintenance of all facilities. Simple agreement between principal and custodial staff appears to be creating conflict in a number of school districts, and staff time also can be wasted.

6. Look at major work schedules to determine how much time should be spent on certain tasks. This issue was addressed in *Public School Survey and Recommendations*, referred to earlier. Establishing uniform time periods required to perform particular tasks should be encouraged.

7. Custodians could work split shifts; that is, they could come to school and open the building, do some preliminary work, go home, and then return to school at the end of the day to do some sweeping. In some school districts, however, custodians must be on hand to watch the operation of a stationary boiler.

8. Clean shops once a week, including home economics rooms. The vocational program areas could be cleaned as part of student training, leaving only maintenance activities to the custodial staff.

9. Science teachers should ask students to clean up the laboratory as part of the program. Equipment should be stored when not in use; custodians should not be expected to work with the equipment due to the possibility of damage.

10. Some of the new floor waxes act as a one-step cleaner and waxer, saving significantly on the cost of stripping floors.

11. Explore the utilization of unemployed individuals to assist with cleaning.

12. Consider asking staff and students to do routine clean up in classrooms. Most students and staff do not come from homes where custodial service is provided. Instead, they are expected to participate in helping with routine maintenance and cleanliness. Why do students, staff, and parents believe that a different standard should be in force at the school? Obviously there are major custodial functions in operating a school facility that can't be handled by students or staff for liability reasons. However, the routine tasks, cleaning up after themselves in classrooms, shop areas, and emptying

smaller trash cans into a larger one could easily be done by students and staff, allowing for reductions in professional custodial help.

## Grounds Use and Maintenance

The community expects to see well-kept grounds; unkempt grounds cause a decrease in real estate values and generally detract from the neighborhood environment. Money can be saved even while grounds are kept to the community's satisfaction.

1. Investigate the feasibility of contracting for grounds maintenance.
2. Explore the utilization of community volunteers to maintain flowerbeds and shrubs on the school grounds.
3. Select low maintenance plantings that are not placed in the way of the lawn mower.
4. Implement an ongoing, efficient program of weed control to avoid problems in this area.
5. Maintain blacktop in good condition; once it is allowed to deteriorate, repairs are costly. A system is needed for regular repair of chuckholes or fractures in the blacktop when they appear.
6. Consider the possibility of allowing large grass fields to go brown during summer months.
7. Install low-maintenance, yet safe, playground apparatus.

## Equipment Use and Maintenance

Maintenance of equipment can be deferred, but this may shorten the life of a given unit. Spending later on capital outlay to replace equipment may be an appropriate cost-saving strategy.

1. When equipment is purchased, find out the availability and cost of expected repairs. These factors, as well as the cost of a maintenance program available to the school district, should be considered when determining purchases.
2. Develop five-year maintenance schedules, updated each year, noting the activities that need to be carried out during that time and the costs associated with those activities. Some items may need repair once every ten years, others on a yearly basis.

3. Keep records on maintenance of repair, using a card file on large items of equipment (purchases costing more than $500). The record on each item will reveal when it should be disposed of; some newer items may need costly repairs, while older items may need little maintenance.
4. Train maintenance staff to repair furniture and equipment. Teach furniture refinishing as part of wood shop course, letting students do the work.
5. A process is needed for reporting possible safety concerns to maintenance staff. Deferring maintenance can result in accidents or lost time; preventive maintenance saves costs.
6. Analyze telephone service, evaluating the need for each extension. Reduce extensions where possible.

### PUPIL TRANSPORTATION

Over the past several years, pupil transportation costs have risen at a rate faster than the Consumer Price Index, and faster than most other segments of the educational program as well. There are three primary reasons for this disproportionate increase: a sharp upswing in fuel costs, rapidly expanding transportation needs for special education, and an increase in the number of school districts offering mandated preschool and or kindergarten programs.

Measures can be taken to reduce expenditures for pupil transportation services, and since the first fuel crisis back in 1973, many districts and bus contractors have taken steps to cut costs. Today, there are dozens of ways to save; some yield immediate results, while others call for "front end" expenditures to bring about savings in the long run. A variety of publications and materials on cutting costs have been produced during the last several years, including the Northwest Energy Education/Management Handbook, which presents short- and long-range ideas for reducing fuel costs.

Other idea resources include the annual summer Pupil Transportation Management workshops, which generally include several sessions on operating transportation systems more efficiently, and school bus newsletters, with their continuous emphasis on cost savings.

Some approaches taken by districts to reduce costs are described below. Any reduction in service should be carefully considered. Above all, safety remains the most important consideration.

**Routes and Schedules**

1. Bus routes should be evaluated periodically to ensure that they are not overlapping one another, and that loading is distributed for greatest efficiency. There are several excellent software packages on the commercial market for routing buses, which use a statistical technique known as regression analysis to recommend the most efficient routes. Check with your state department of education pupil transportation specialist for more details.
2. Larger buses and longer routes may be a consideration.
3. Deadhead mileage can be reduced by adding bus storage areas.
4. Staggering schedules allows for better utilization of buses and drivers.
5. In a district with a large enrollment in a relatively compact geographic area, staggering class schedules allows for better use of buses and driver time. Less is spent on equipment, storage areas, insurance, drivers' wages and benefits, training and licensing. A large suburban district found that the number of buses used could be reduced 20 percent through rerouting and by staggering the elementary school starting/dismissal times by one-half hour.
6. A small district covering a large geographic area could eliminate early afternoon routes for primary grade students. While staff and parents may protest the longer school day, the cost advantages are obvious.
7. Scheduling all students for one regular dismissal time can eliminate the need for duplicate runs.
8. Schedule kindergarten students to travel home with older students or eliminate noon runs and ask parents to be responsible for picking up students. Daylong kindergarten on alternating days could be considered, as well as a four-day school week for primary students.
9. Increasing students' walking distance to school and bus stops, while felt by many to be the best way to cut costs, may prove highly controversial, especially in the area of safeguarding students from potential traffic hazards.

**Activity Trips**

1. The number of trips can be reduced; trips and events can be coordinated so that buses carry full loads.

2. Establishing the minimum and maximum distances allowed for field trips, and making each educational unit or program responsible for trip expenses, can yield savings.
3. Use a Telexplorer, an amplified telephone developed for conference calls, as a viable alternative to field trips, or use two-way interactive video/television to conduct the virtual field trip instead of actually traveling to the site.
4. Consider cutting all field trips.
5. Take a serious look at reducing athletic and other extracurricular activity travel costs. If your school plays 2.5 to 3 hours away, do all of the teams play the same day and go on the same bus? Costs are $250–$300 per trip or more, and we wouldn't spend that much somewhere else without a pretty comprehensive review. The same would go for things like FFA trips. Assuming you have an FFA, when your FFA chapter goes to a state convention or the state fair, do you travel as a league or with each school? It may make more economic sense for several neighboring schools to all ride on the same bus and to share costs to some events versus going alone.
6. Consider cutting professional training travel, including board travel costs. Wouldn't it be fun if someone chartered a bus to the state school boards convention in your state, by starting in remote areas and districts in your county and region, and picking up board members from separate districts as it travels across the county and region eventually getting to the final destination? This might become a yearly event that people would look forward to and enjoy and the districts would be able to share the costs of travel.

## School Bus Operation

1. Some states still have union high school districts. Small component districts in a union high district can consolidate fleets; for example, some districts operate on a cooperative basis, others contract with the union high district for services, while still others utilize a single bus contractor in common.
2. Convert from gasoline to propane, or gasoline to diesel.
3. Investigate the feasibility of contracting for bus service.
4. Insurance programs should be reviewed and all options investigated for reduced costs for coverage. Consider bidding bus fleet insurance.

## Driver Training

1. Driving for fuel economy can produce surprising cost savings. Two fleets utilizing a system for drivers trained in fuel economy will save 10–15 percent in fuel costs.
2. Promote good driving habits: shorter warm-up periods, smooth starts and stops, driving at steady speeds, and so forth.
3. Use deadhead route mileage and time for driver training; experienced drivers can assist with behind-the-wheel training for new drivers.
4. Consider eliminating driver education altogether, subcontracting these services, or teaching behind-the-wheel programs in the summer time only.

## Equipment and Maintenance

1. Purchase equipment that provides for the least expense over its entire life. Diesel-powered equipment costs more to purchase, but significantly less in terms of fuel and maintenance; many diesel fleets are realizing 40–50 percent reductions in fuel costs, and a considerable reduction in maintenance costs. A thorough study of engine types and sizes in terms of servicing needs also can prove cost effective.
2. Even though an initial investment for radial tires is more than for other types of tires, some districts have found them cost effective in terms of increased mileage and reduced fuel and maintenance costs.
3. Electronic ignition systems can reduce maintenance costs by lengthening ignition component life. One district recouped its initial investment within two years.

## FOOD SERVICES

Increasing program costs (purchased foods, supplies, wages, and fringe benefits) continue to force per meal costs up in school nutrition programs. However, charging more for meals is not acceptable to parents, especially in this period of high unemployment and declining income. Given the choice of charging higher prices or underwriting additional costs through the budget, districts have taken a variety of approaches to find a solution.

- Programs can operate on a totally self-supporting basis.
- They can operate within an established budget.
- The district can establish a per meal cost and underwrite all costs above that figure.
- The district can underwrite all costs as a part of the total expense of educating students and serve meals at no charge to students.
- The district may choose to not offer a program.

In operating a nutrition program, a balance between expenses and income may be found by reviewing present practices, and possibly modifying and updating procedures.

1. Plan menus to make full use of commodities. Do a menu item cost analysis and reduce the frequency that high cost items appear on the menu. Cost account the entire menu to establish a balance between production costs and income. Utilize cycle menus, preferably seventeen-day cycles. Menus that include a high frequency of prefab or convenience (processed) items cut sharply into a district's ability to use commodity foods (especially bonus commodity) cost effectively.

2. Purchase food from a planned menu cycle. Purchase in quantity, as much as storage will allow economically. Avoid "settling in" with one supplier for convenience, as this can be costly. Shop for good prices; food suppliers are in a competitive business and schools represent very desirable accounts.

3. For a cost-effective program, three types of storage areas are needed: frozen, cold, and dry. Keep inventories in each area current as food is received and used. Store items most often used toward the entrance, least used in the rear. A security system will help avoid losses. Temperature controls for the frozen and cold storage areas should be safeproofed. Mice, insects, and dampness contaminate food, and precautions are relatively inexpensive when compared to the costs of food lost.

4. A good cost-accounting system is essential; otherwise, large and unexpected deficits may occur. Cost accounting must be done at the building level, through the food service director and business manager. Building-level managers, once informed and involved, can play a major role in controlling costs and maintaining quality.

5. Many school districts in Oregon, for example, have "turned around" their school food service programs with the help of the film training program, "Efficient School Food Production." This series is available from all ESDs at no cost to districts. The films provide training in every skill necessary for the preparation of quality foods. Some districts are considering this training as a prerequisite to employment and salary increases. It is timely, appropriate, and indeed a financial necessity that classified food service personnel contracts include unpaid training requirements.

6. Production records are the best safeguard from the over- and underproduction of food. Overproduction drives up per meal costs; underproduction reduces income and discourages participation. Production records are essential to accurate planning. They are an excellent communication tool between the building-level manager, district food service director, business manager, and superintendent. The records also are an excellent way for certifying compliance with federal, state, and local standards as to portion size.

7. Full use of USDA donated commodities, regular and bonus, is resulting in 36% per meal savings in some districts. Others utilize commodities at a much less per meal rate, which increases their per meal costs significantly.

8. A lunch period that is truly a lunch period is advisable. Scheduling numerous activities at that time decreases participation in the lunch program. The lunch period should be long enough to allow time for all students to be served and to eat. The staggering of lunch periods has helped increase student participation in the school nutrition program of many schools. And the food service program will become an integral part of the total educational program when students are helped to learn good nutrition habits.

9. When pricing meals, students should be charged the actual cost of per meal preparation less the total of (a) state matching per meal revenue plus (b) federal per meal reimbursement plus (c) federal com-

modity per meal value. If the local school district elects to underwrite a portion of the cost, that too should be deducted from the price established for the paying student. All adults should be charged at least the actual cost of per meal preparation. For example: if five adult employees eat lunch at $3.00 per day (actual per meal cost of preparation), the cost to the district (5 x $3.00 x 183) is $2,745.00 per year.

10. School districts should avoid having income siphoned from school food services to others during the lunch period, such as student stores, vending machines, or food sales, especially if you wish to run an operation in the black.

11. School nutrition program income comes from basically five sources: monies from paying students and adults, federal reimbursement, federal donated commodities, state matching monies, and local school district subsidy. Increased average daily participation increases income in the first four categories. "Good food and good service" are the keys to increasing participation.


## EXPANDED COST-SAVING IDEAS

### Buildings and Grounds: Expanded Idea #1

Often, several buildings in a school district are open on the same night, with only a minimum of student or community activities scheduled for each. Scheduling activities in the fewest number of buildings practicable saves custodial and energy costs. However, you may wish to continue the practice of scheduling activities in the neighborhood elementary school if the activity is serving the needs of students enrolled exclusively in that school.

*Advantages:* Makes best use of one or a few buildings; encourages better supervision and security; reduces energy costs for light and fuel, and reduces custodial costs; improves public relations with special custodians and supervisory personnel in the buildings used; less disruption of the cleaning schedule in schools used least. Consider installing a graveyard shift at the high school. One person could be on duty during the day who oversees boilers and the lunch area, another crew can begin cleaning classrooms in the evening and handle night events, and a more focused, deep-cleaning crewperson can come on after the building closes for the night, allowing this person to spend 100 percent of his or her time cleaning without interruptions. It is a very efficient system and it will reduce vandalism since the building is occupied twenty-four hours per day.

*Disadvantages:* Increases wear and tear on buildings used most frequently; creates public inconvenience in terms of distances traveled; requires more administrative time for scheduling; creates parking problems when facilities used are limited; may incur comment that facilities in a certain school are not readily available.

*Additional Information:* The building(s) assigned to night utilization could be cleaned on a graveyard work shift. The swing shift custodian would be given special training for handling public groups. Senior high schools have both specialized and general use areas. There are fewer specialized areas in junior high and elementary schools. A graduated fee schedule could be initiated, with a higher charge at the schools designated for minimum night use and a lower charge for the maximum night-use schools. Charges should be established realistically on the basis of actual cost analysis. Reduced rates to special groups actually subsidizes those groups through tax dollars. Activities for children, such as Scouting and Campfire, may be given special consideration, but check court cases relating to if you allow one group to use your facility you may also have to allow all such groups to use your facility.

## Building and Grounds: Expanded Idea #2

Lease or rent surplus building space. Declining school populations in many districts mean that some school buildings are not being used to their capacities. Extra income can be earned by school districts if they rent or lease the vacant space in these school buildings.

*Advantages:* Earns extra income; uses all available space; the public perceives the district as making "good use" of available resources.

*Disadvantages:* Renting out space may reduce available program options; the mixing of uses may not be compatible; and the costs incurred when renting the space may be greater than the income.

*Additional Information:* The potential earning power of a given space depends upon such factors as parking, building age, and location. Contact a local commercial real estate firm for estimates of earning potential.

## Building and Grounds: Expanded Idea #3

Equipment and facilities owned by school districts should be maintained according to a five-year schedule.

*Advantages:* Avoids costly breakdowns of equipment or building closures; uses resources more efficiently; extends equipment and building life.

*Disadvantages:* Staff time required to operate the program may be more costly than the results; schedules may not be adhered to during times of diminishing resources.

## Transportation: Expanded Idea #4

Many fleets in Oregon, for example, are purchasing diesel-powered buses whenever replacement or additional vehicles are needed. Converting existing buses from gasoline to diesel does not appear to be feasible, except for the larger, transit-type buses.

*Advantages:* Yields 50 to 100 percent more miles per gallon. Several fleets claim between two and three times the number of miles with diesel for each hour of engine maintenance. Cost of fuel is generally lower; 25 to 50 percent fuel cost reduction; maintenance costs are lower; engine life is longer, especially with high mileage usage.

*Disadvantages:* Initial cost is high: a diesel engine can cost from $3,600 to $6,000 more than a gas-powered engine. However, districts indicate an eighteen- to thirty-six-month payback. The additional weight may require heavier suspension components. Heavier components, however, should provide a savings over the lifetime of the bus. In addition, mechanics may need retraining; additional fueling equipment may be required; and fumes and engine noise can prove objectionable.

*Additional Information:* Information is available from manufacturers of midrange diesels; fleet operators who have been using diesel-powered equipment also can be consulted.

## Transportation: Expanded Idea #5

During the past several years, several fleets have converted some of their buses from gasoline fuel to propane, and most indicate that properly converted vehicles yield cost savings. There are many regulations, approvals, and permits that are required when converting to propane, and there is some concern that propane's price advantage will be reduced if natural gas is deregulated by the federal government.

*Advantages:* Fuel costs are reduced by 20 to 40 percent; propane has a higher octane rating than gasoline; propane is a cleaner burning fuel, resulting in fewer pollutants; engine components and oil last longer.

*Disadvantages:* "Front end" cost to convert vehicles; conversion can affect vehicle warranty and product liability. Reports indicate 5 to 20 percent less mileage per gallon of fuel; some drivers have indicated a small power loss, particularly on hills. Additional fueling facility is required; training is needed for maintenance personnel and those responsible for fueling buses; and there may be a problem locating fueling stations while en route.

*Additional Information:* Costs for conversion can run from $1,600 to $2,800 per vehicle. Reports indicate recouping initial conversion costs between one and two and one-half years after conversion. Propane storage tank and fueling equipment required; costs vary according to tank size and location. Regulations and information regarding installation requirements can be obtained from the state fire marshal's office and your state department's pupil transportation services office.

## Transportation: Expanded Idea #6

Additional starting and dismissal times allow for increased utilization of existing buses, resulting in significant savings. This is effective mainly for schools that have attendance areas small enough to allow for trips to be completed in forty minutes or less and that have a sufficient number of students to fill the buses.

*Advantages:* Better utilization of buses; reduced service levels for students not necessary; produces immediate cost savings without initial implementation cost; less equipment and storage needed.

*Disadvantages:* Rescheduling the starting and dismissal times can result in reactions from staff, students, and parents; complaints may arise if pickup or drop-off times are scheduled during winter months when it is dark.

*Additional Information:* Costs significantly reduced, less new equipment needed, lower cost for driver licensing and training, possible savings on drivers' wages and benefits. Several districts have utilized this approach to reduce transportation costs; one large metropolitan district hopes to cut back on regular route buses by approximately 20 percent. Professional consultants are available to review programs and suggest cost-savings measures. General information can be obtained from your state department's pupil transportation services office.

## Transportation: Expanded Idea #7

Consolidation of fleets is an approach used by several districts to reduce transportation costs; this is particularly effective in union high school districts or in relatively small geographic areas where there are two or more adjoining districts. Combining bus fleets on a contractual or cooperative basis allows for the use of equipment on regularly scheduled routes by more than one district. For example, several Washington school districts including Centralia and Chehalis are the key partners in a transportation cooperative.

*Advantages:* Reduction in the number of buses needed; increased utilization of equipment; can increase the size of a fleet to justify the employment of full-time transportation supervisory personnel and to operate an effective bus maintenance program; more efficient use of drivers' time; can save on driver training expense by utilizing just one certified driver trainer to serve the entire fleet.

*Disadvantages:* Possible changes in starting and dismissal times; lack of flexibility for individual schools due to the need to coordinate route schedules; possible difficulty in determining component share of transportation expense; could limit the number of buses available for extra trips; possible negative reactions from staff and parents if schedules are changed.

*Additional Information:* Agreements or contracts need to be negotiated to establish operational responsibilities and methods for determining respective costs.

In almost every instance, there has been a reduction in overall cost for transportation service without increased expenses to implement the program. Districts that have consolidated fleets or contracted services are the best resource for information.

## Transportation: Expanded Idea #8

Since only certain types of pupil transportation are required, it is possible to eliminate most of the school bus programs in the majority of districts; at least two districts have done this in recent years. Because an average of only half of a typical district's students are transported, most districts can muster a majority to support the elimination of pupil transportation when this is legal to do in your state. However, in some districts where transportation has been eliminated or walking distances have been extended significantly, parent reaction has been strong, especially during winter months. Since state school support reimburses local districts for approximately 70 percent of approved transportation costs, eliminating programs results in a savings of only 30 cents on the dollar.

*Advantages:* Can save the taxpayers approximately 30 cents on each dollar spent for transportation.

*Disadvantages:* Due to the transportation apportionment law, savings would not be realized until the second year following curtailment; can result in strong adverse parental reaction, particularly when students are denied transportation or are required to walk greater distances to bus stops; can split parental support for schools, as only half of the student population will be affected in the typical district; can cause political problems if transportation is curtailed and the athletic program is retained; possible hardships for families without access to transportation or funds to pay for transportation; more fuel and energy required if parents transport students on an individual or carpool basis.

*Additional Information:* Information can be obtained from schools that have eliminated regular school transportation services across the country.

## ENERGY CONSERVATION IN SCHOOL TRANSPORTATION

Energy conservation in school transportation is a major area of concern to the educational community. School buses travel in excess of four billion miles annually, consuming 900 million gallons of fuel and transporting 55 percent of the school enrollment.

Since the energy crisis descended, school transportation managers have initiated efforts to reduce the amount of fuel required to operate their fleets. Rapidly escalating fuel prices and limited school budgets are forcing a strong stand for conserving energy. Here are 101 ways transportation can conserve energy and reduce transportation costs.

## Transportation Policy

1. Coordinate school calendars and start and dismissal times between schools of each school system.
2. Eliminate staggered dismissal times in the same building.
3. Increase requirements for walking distances to school and to bus stops.
4. Establish take-up and dismissal schedules at schools to support maximum vehicle utilization.
5. Eliminate buses for detention students.
6. Limit student parking, encourage high school pupils to ride school buses, form car pools, and similar programs.
7. For districts or schools that are close together geographically, establish maximum distances for cocurricular trips (for example, 60 miles round trip).
8. Utilize public mass transit where feasible to avoid duplication of service.
9. Establish travel restrictions for school-sponsored activities supporting athletic teams (cheerleaders, band, pep clubs, rooters, etc.).
10. Eliminate buses for athletic team practices.

## School Bus Operation: Activity and Field Trips

11. Reduce or eliminate all but the most necessary athletic contests.
12. Reduce or eliminate all but the most necessary cocurricular trips.
13. Combine cocurricular and athletic trips for more than one school.
14. Have districts share buses when feasible.
15. Establish minimum and maximum distances for all trips.
16. Limit cocurricular trips to full busloads only.
17. Combine athletic schedules so several games can be played at the same time.
18. Encourage parents to pool with other parents in transporting children to school for late activities and for extracurricular activities.

19. Contract with parents to provide transportation when feasible, but check on the liabilities involved with your legal counsel and insurance carrier or agent of record.
20. Utilize public transportation on return trips where feasible rather than return school buses to schools or homes.

## School Bus Operation: General

21. Lengthen distances between pickup points.
22. Establish collection points.
23. Plan stops on level areas instead of on inclines.
24. Consolidate loads.
25. Plan routes to make only right-hand turns, to save on idling time, where safety permits.
26. Use intercoms and cameras on buses to reduce stops for controlling discipline.
27. Install trip recorders to record and monitor driver and vehicle operation when necessary.
28. Use smallest available vehicle for long distance, light-load runs.
29. Install two-way radios to direct operation or redirection of buses to avoid unnecessary use.
30. Route buses to stay on main roads as much as possible.

## School Bus Routing and Scheduling

31. Fill buses to legal capacity.
32. When replacing buses or expanding fleet, purchase buses with capacities to provide balanced fleet utilization.
33. Utilize proven updating routing techniques, either by hand or computer, to maintain maximum vehicle utilization at all times.

   • Evaluate current system.
   • Revise system to reduce mileage, stops, and student riding time and distance.
   • Review policy and revise where needed.

34. Consolidate interdistrict transportation systems when possible to meet special transportation demands.

35. Develop an alternate routing plan for implementation in emergencies and fuel shortages.

## School Bus Operation: The Driver

36. Retain experienced drivers as long as possible.
37. Reeducate bus drivers toward better fuel economy.
38. Reduce warm-up time on buses to two minutes initially, and three minutes prior to starting routes. Driver should dress warmer rather than running engines at full idle to heat buses.
39. Drive slowly the first few miles until vehicle warms up.
40. Avoid full-throttle operation. Drive at steady speeds.
41. Avoid the "red line," even in shifting gears.
42. Drive slowly back to bus garage. Turn corners slowly.
43. Reduce speed limit to as low as practical.
44. Avoid courtesy (unauthorized) stops.
45. Train new drivers on existing runs while bus is "deadheading."
46. Use simulators to reduce behind-the-wheel training in vehicles.
47. Increase frequency of driver in-service programs.
48. Hold joint workshops with drivers and mechanics to improve transportation operation.
49. Use an incentive system for reducing vehicle fuel consumption.
50. Review driver times and routes. Determine most efficient vehicle utilization, layover, and storage plans to minimize miles for school as well as personal vehicles.
51. Keep foot off accelerator when the bus is stopped and off brakes when in motion. Reduce braking by anticipating stops.

## School Bus Maintenance

52. Tune and maintain engines, plugs, points, and timing.
53. Maintain and clean pollution controls.
54. Keep gas tanks full to avoid excessive evaporation.
55. Avoid fuel spillage when refueling buses. Do not overfill.
56. Replace buses that use excessive amounts of fuel as soon as economically feasible.
57. Keep gasoline tanks locked with one person in charge of fueling of buses and other school vehicles.

58. Keep accurate bus records for maintenance and fuel consumption.
59. Analyze record data for potential management decisions to achieve savings.
60. Inventory all parts and supplies and order for a full year on a planned-need basis, with best price on past experiences (reduces "parts chasing").
61. In winter keep all buses under cover rather than allowing drivers to take home and park.
62. Use engine warmers for easier starts.
63. Maintain clean oil and air filters.
64. Keep automatic choke clean. A sticking choke will waste fuel.
65. Keep air-fuel mixture or carburetor precisely adjusted.
66. Regulate oil change with engine tune-up.
67. Use manufacturer's recommended weight of oil. A heavier oil will force the engine to use more fuel, too light will not provide the protection required.
68. Check tire balance and wheel alignment to avoid "drag," which will use more fuel and shorten tire life.
69. Check radiator thermostat. A defective thermostat may prolong engine warm-up, increasing fuel consumption.
70. Use proper octane-rated fuel. Using wrong octane will result in plug foul-up and reduction of mileage. Using a higher octane than required is a waste of money.
71. Use engine-analyzing equipment to assure maximum efficiency.
72. Make full utilization of service manuals and maintenance bulletins to keep updated on maintenance techniques.
73. Take full advantage of free maintenance training clinics conducted by skilled instructors.
74. Keep brakes properly adjusted.
75. Repair engine oil leaks.
76. Install radiator shutters for retaining engine heat.
77. Install radial tires.
78. Retrofit ignition with electronic ignition system.
79. Properly utilize proven fuel and oil additives.
80. Maintain proper tire pressure.
81. Utilize new techniques such as rubber suspension systems, wheel balancers, tire pressure equalizers, solid state ignition, and so forth.

### Transportation Office and Garage

82. Maintain lighting fixtures (a clean fixture in good working order can deliver up to 50 percent more light).
83. Clean walls and ceilings and/or paint with light flat or semigloss finish.
84. Turn off all lights and other electrical equipment when not in use.
85. Reduce exterior lighting to lowest level consistent with good security and safety.
86. Perform janitorial services earlier so that electricity may be turned off earlier.
87. Check all equipment and motors. Adjust belts for proper tension; turn off when not in use.
88. Limit the use of electrical space heaters.
89. Tighten and clean all electrical connections from the circuit breakers back through the transformers to the main switch (should be done annually by an experienced electrician when building power is off).
90. Consider the installation of photocell controllers to turn exterior lights on and off.
91. Concentrate evening work/meetings in a single heating/cooling zone instead of heating or cooling the whole office or garage.
92. Clean up heat exchanger and heating oil surfaces for better heat transfer, change filters at regular intervals, clean fan blades and damper blades.
93. Request visitors and staff to avoid introduction of adverse conditions by opening windows or holding open doors.
94. Consider the installation of added insulation to building walls and ceiling to decrease heat transfer.
95. Consider the installation of insulating glass in place of single pane glass.
96. Consider the installation of weather-stripping, caulking, automatic door closers, and so on to decrease infiltration of outside air.
97. Close off all unnecessary openings—unused exhaust fans, broken windows, structural openings.
98. Replace grossly oversized motors. Motors operate more efficiently near rated capacity and with a better power factor.

99. Utilize blower system to circulate warm air from the ceiling to floor of work areas.
100. Remove thermostats located near doors, windows, or heat-producing sources.
101. Reduce thermostat setting on weekends, holidays, and at night.

## CUT COSTS CREATIVELY WITH VIDEOCONFERENCING

With cuts in federal funds, state school fund support, and recent levy and tax base failures, educators are asked to reduce expenses without a loss of quality in the education being delivered. Field trips and travel are areas that have been particularly vulnerable to increased costs and, as a consequence, vulnerable to budget cuts. Yet these are important to the education of your students and the administration of your district.

There is a way to reduce field trip and travel costs significantly without giving up the benefits of either. How? By applying the concept of Telexplorer, V-Tel, or conference calls on phones using telephone equipment designed for use with groups, like classes or groups of teachers, to replace some or all field trips and travel to meetings. What makes this equipment practical is its low cost, portability, and effectiveness.

Field trips cost, on the average, between $250 and $300 each or more depending on distance to the site. These trips are often more expensive, or impractical, for rural districts because of the time, distance, and cost involved. Field trips by conference phone, V-Tel, or Telexplorer are not designed to directly replace all trips. For example, a trip to the coast for students from eastern Oregon could not be replaced with conference calls, V-Tel, or Telexplorer. However, if the budget did not have room for the trip, a call to a regional oceanographer or coastal fishing company would serve to educate students about problems facing the coast.

Conference calls, V-Tel, and the Telexplorer work best when they make completely new experiences possible. A class in government gains new insights when they talk to their legislators in Salem, Oregon, or Washington, D.C., visits that travel time and cost would otherwise make impossible. V-Tel, Telexplorer, and conference calls can become an integral part of the curriculum. For example, an English class reads and discusses a book. They also discuss how a writer writes. The next step is a V-Tel, Telexplorer, or conference call to the author. Students have prepared for this so they can ask questions about writing and the book. The call could be followed up with a creative writing project using what they learned talking to the author.

V-Tel, Telexplorer, and conference calls must be a planned tool to be effective, just like any field trip. It is a very cost-effective way to bring resources to the classroom. People active in specific fields related to curriculum, professionals for career education, and college placement officials are just some of the resources available with V-Tel, conference calls, and Telexplorer.

The telephone equipment is simple to use, portable, easy to set up, and most important, inexpensive. A portable conference telephone that includes a speaker and two external microphones designed for use with classroom-sized groups currently leases for less than $15 a month. Your only other expense is the cost of any long distance calls, which varies from company to company within and between states.

V-Tel equipment, though a little more sophisticated and expensive, allows a school to regain its initial investment by cutting the cost of travel. Video-conference phones over the Internet should also be used.

To manage costs, it is vital that districts maximize all available resources. This includes the conference call, V-Tel, and Telexplorer program. The program can reduce travel costs associated with district administration. Administrative meetings, meetings with consultants, staff interviews, and in-service training can all be done with the conference call, V-Tel, or Telexplorer equipment. This reduces costs associated with those meeting while maximizing one of your most cost-effective resources.

The benefits extend beyond the important dollar savings. Time is saved, thereby improving productivity. People who are out of town could still attend an important meeting via conference calls, V-Tel, or Telexplorer. Depending on your district's needs, remote and homebound instruction could be added to your program.

Most of your major phone companies provide this service, as well as materials and training necessary for a successful conference call, V-Tel, and Telexplorer program. Call your local phone company service providers for more information or contact your regional education service district provider.

Incidentally, the Internet and computers outfitted with phones and two-way cameras can also serve the same function as phone conferences,

V-Tel, and Telexplorers, and they also provide an image of the person you are speaking with. Such devices are now available for a relatively low cost and can be carried in the palm of your hand.

Distance-learning technologies such as these add relevance to the discussion and make sense with respect to cost savings. Phone conferences, V-Tel, Telexplorers, and videophones are a huge replacement for expensive field trips. It is one thing to talk on the phone, but V-Tel can take your students visually to many places they have never been, motivate them, and add meaning and engagement to their interactions, which will truly activate student learning and achievement.

## CASE STUDY EXAMPLES

### Classified Employees

In searching for cost-saving initiatives, agencies sometimes overlook assets they already have at their disposal, including human capital. For some school districts, that capital comes in the form of classified employees who are being underutilized.

These are individuals who may have hidden talents and capabilities that have never been recognized. Much of the underlying philosophy behind this initiative can be found in the term *empowerment*. At the Umatilla-Morrow Education Service District, employees are offered what are called "growth opportunities." These are special projects or assignments beyond the normal duties and expectations for employees.

Some employees run with these growth opportunities while others become overwhelmed and provide a reminder that "their plate is already too full," or suggest that they are simply too stretched to add anything further, or they simply can't deliver. It becomes something of a natural sorting process or a way of identifying those who should be empowered. Some examples in this arena include:

*The Receptionist*

Several years ago, when the ESD was faced with possible layoffs due to state budget cuts, a group of employees asked what they could do to help keep their jobs. The answer was simple, "Make sure you are essential."

One of the most inventive was the receptionist who had primarily answered the telephone and greeted visitors although she was always willing to help where needed since she sometimes had periods of downtime. Within a year of the message, she took over the homeschool program, became editor of the in-house employee newsletter, began ordering monogrammed clothing for the 270 employees, took over the assistive technology distribution program, took on oversight of two Forest Service facilities that are used by school districts and community groups through an ESD contract, and several other projects—all while continuing as the receptionist.

## The Substitute Caller

Some years ago, the Walla Walla School District, Walla Walla, Washington, hired a new substitute caller who had been working as a receptionist at a local bank. Her primary duty was to call substitutes for a school district of 6,000 students and a nearby district of 1,000 students. Several other departments that interfaced with this individual regarding substitutes were short-handed. Before long, it became apparent that she was capable of more.

Within a year after her employment, the substitute caller became much more, although she remained in her classified clerical position. She began taking care of the payroll for all substitutes, began taking applications and reviewing credentials, assembled evaluative reports from schools, and in short, essentially took care of every aspect of work related to substitutes. While she received a modest bump in salary, her primary interest was in greater job satisfaction and more meaningful work.

## The Medicaid/Administrative Billing Clerks

In May 2004, the board was reviewing summer travel requests and noted that two clerks who process Medicaid/Administrative billing for the ESD were scheduled to go to the national conference and training session for people with this responsibility. The event was scheduled for Boston.

They were a bit surprised, since this program had been under the direction of the assistant superintendent and everyone assumed that she or someone at that level would be attending. They quickly learned that these two individuals had taken over the program entirely and would be the ones who ought to participate.

Said one of the individuals, "When the assistant superintendent asked if I would like to try working in this area, I was pretty skeptical because it looked like something beyond me. I would have to deal with a very complex program and train people all over the ESD, including teachers, principals, and superintendents. But she told me she had faith in me and thought I could do it so I gave it a try."

The second individual came from Great Britain with a military husband and came to work at the ESD doing very basic support assignments. She too was asked if she would like to try her hand at something more complex, which led her to a full-time assignment supporting school districts with the Medicaid Billing.

One night she was asked to make a presentation to the board of education—something she had never done. She scheduled an appointment with someone in the Instructional Services Department and got information about a basic lesson plan. In putting together her presentation, she followed the basic lesson plan format in helping the board better understand a very complex program or concept. It was very possibly one of the most effective presentations the board had ever heard and served once again as a reminder that most school districts could save management costs by simply providing classified staff with expanded opportunities and utilizing some natural talent that remains untapped within the organization.

## Custodians

### The Graveyard Shift

In many school districts, the most expensive custodians are generally those who work the day shift while those at the entry level work at night.

At one very large high school, the head custodian worked by himself during the day. He had an engaging personality and was popular with students and staff as he moved around the building. Since the building was full while he was on duty, he was limited in what he could actually do in terms of cleaning and maintenance. And while he was the head custodian, he had little contact with those who worked in his department.

The night shift employees, who were actually supervised on-the-job by the assistant custodian, were able to focus more intensely on cleaning and maintenance since the building was less occupied outside of school hours. Still, with night activities and constant interruptions, cleaning was not efficient.

The school had a total of six custodians since it was a very large building. When the assistant custodian retired and a vacancy emerged, district officials decided to restructure the assignments and create greater efficiencies. The first thing they did was move the assistant custodian to a graveyard shift. They also had two other custodians assigned to the graveyard shift working with the assistant custodian. Because the building was empty during their shift, their efficiency almost doubled.

When an opening came for a head custodian, that individual was assigned to the late afternoon/night shift so that it would overlap with the day shift and the graveyard shift. A day person was assigned to be on-site while students and staff were in the building. Because of the efficiencies experienced by this model, the total staffing went from six to five.

## Contracting: Part One

Much of the work of the Education Service District involves contracting to do work for others based upon a regional concept that reflects efficiencies based upon scale. In looking at its maintenance and custodial needs, the ESD concluded that what's good for the goose might also be good for the gander.

The ESD is located in Pendleton, which has a school district of about 3,500 students and both a maintenance and custodial staff. The ESD, with much more limited building space, was trying to satisfy its maintenance and custodial needs with one day person and a part-time night staffer. The ESD did not have the equipment or the specialized personnel to handle its maintenance needs, which were being contracted out to private vendors at rates of $75 an hour or more.

The Pendleton School District was contacted and asked if it would be interested in contracting to provide maintenance and custodial services for the ESD—essentially treating the ESD office as just another "education site."

The district agreed and began providing custodians. The district also began responding to maintenance needs by using district staffers with specialties in electrical, carpentry, plumbing, and so forth. The result has been both a cost saving and much better facility management. In addition, the contract expands the maintenance and custodial budget for the district, which also expands the scope of the service model they can make available to their regular school buildings.

## Contracting: Part Two

Some local school districts are contracting out custodial services in one of two ways—to a nearby, larger school district or to a private custodial and maintenance firm.

While the contract with a larger school district or other education entity is still rare, it offers an opportunity for savings and efficiencies as well as expanded service possibilities.

Contracting with a private firm offers greater staffing flexibility and reduces the oversight burden for school personnel—in much the same way that this approach has become popular for dealing with food services and transportation.

## Food Purchasing Cooperatives

The director of food services for the Umatilla School District, Umatilla, Oregon, and the director of the UMESD Intermountain Cooperative had been involved in numerous discussions and had long believed that small districts needed to find a way to lower their food costs. In response, a core group of school districts gathered (Pilot Rock SD, Morrow County SD, Echo SD, Milton-Freewater SD, Helix SD, and Athena-Weston SD) and put together a proposal to school districts in eastern Oregon to address their food service needs. Representatives from districts around eastern Oregon were invited to a special meeting to ascertain interest. This occurred in the spring of 2004. The turnout was well beyond expectations.

A number of the school districts indicated a desire to become part of a food-purchasing cooperative and they spent the spring and summer of 2004 putting together a bid to encompass any school districts in eastern Oregon that wanted to join the cooperative. One of the strong points of the bid was to find a supplier willing to service small districts scattered across a remote area.

Such a supplier was located and a bid was awarded. The new food-purchasing cooperative went into effect in the fall of 2004 with districts enjoying significant savings on their food purchases.

The Umatilla food service director also contracts to oversee the Ione School District food service program. While there is a cook on-site in Ione, he oversees food purchases, helps with menu planning, shares creative ideas for increasing participation, and handles all of the state and federal reporting requirements.

## Cutting Shipping Costs

Hill Meat Company, located in Pendleton, Oregon, sends trucks on an almost daily basis to such metropolitan centers as Portland, Seattle, and Boise. The trucks have historically returned to Pendleton empty. The Intermountain Purchasing Cooperative contacted Hill Meat Company and was able to negotiate a transportation contract that helped the Hill Meat Company offset its costs of returning the trucks to Pendleton while also providing a regular source of trucking for the purchasing cooperative. An added bonus of this contract has been the fact that the cooperative worked out an arrangement with the Northwest Textbook Depository for hauling textbooks to area schools in eastern Oregon. Due to the weight of such shipments, the savings on the overall cost of new textbooks has been tremendous.

There are probably many communities that have either regular trucking firms or businesses that are sending trucks to assorted locations. With the costs of gasoline continuing to rise and with shipping costs becoming higher and higher, it pays to form a partnership with those entities, which can make a contribution to their local schools by hauling supplies, equipment, and instructional materials and helping save shipping costs.

## The Maintenance Review, Ione School District, Ione, Oregon

About six months after the Ione School District was formed, the board's Facility and Grounds Committee conducted a complete walk-through along with the site administrator, the head custodian, the superintendent, and the facility consultant. In addition, staff members were asked to identify anything in their area that needed attention. Custodians also made a list. The items ranged everywhere from needing new boilers and bleachers to a broken drinking fountain or a lock that might need attention.

Once the list was complete, the tasks were divided up among a variety of individuals. Several local residents who were off during the winter and interested in doing odd jobs were hired by the hour to work down the list. At one point during the holiday break, there were seven people working in the building. A reference list of personnel included:

Loyal Burns—a local resident licensed to do electrical work and assorted other projects. Loyal is on-call to the district at a set rate.

Tom Brandon—a retired school administrator who is an expert on school facilities and who is retained by the district as a consultant, as was Bob DePoe who helped oversee completion of the new elementary school.

Maintenance—This includes the custodians as well as several local residents who agreed to work part time for the district helping with various repairs, including Mark Bruno. The others were paid by the hour to address the items on the list: Kelly Giffith, head custodian; George Murdock, the superintendent; Dick Allen, the site administrator; and John and Gregg, the two board members who are the Facilities & Grounds Committee.

The results of the walk-through produced a long list of items that needed attention. The list is being included in its entirety to demonstrate the comprehensive nature of the project. Six months after the list was created, every item identified during the walk-through had been addressed. As one might expect, a number of the items on the list had been problems for years. Being a small district, Ione was in no position to maintain a permanent staff to handle maintenance issues. The creation of a short-term maintenance team—at a relatively low cost—enabled the district to fix, repair, or replace every single item that was in need of attention. It also provided a short-term source of employment for local citizens who needed something to occupy their time.

The district will continue with its walk-through concept every six months, although it is quite unlikely that it will ever be necessary to create such a long list of items needing attention.

The district has not invested in equipment for maintaining the outside of the school facilities. The City of Ione purchased a new $30,000 mower and the district is contracting for mowing and watering services using city employees at a fraction of what it might take to either hire regular staff or to purchase and maintain equipment.

When the district has need of tractors or similar items of equipment, community members and board members who serve on the Facility & Grounds Committee bring in the necessary equipment from their farms or private businesses.

**Table 4.1.   Immediate Repair List**

| | |
|---|---|
| Move mirror in North Hall boys bathroom and paint | Maintenance |
| Base molding in gym under and around mats | Maintenance |
| Cover steam pipe in gym | Maintenance |
| Repair gym bleachers | Maintenance |
| Check, replace bulbs in all exterior lights | Kelly |
| Check clothes dryer operation | Maintenance |
| Build step in boiler room to electrical panel | Maintenance |
| Put grate back on stage wall | Maintenance |
| Repair benches in cafeteria | Maintenance |
| Replace mirror in boys' bathroom (Dick will order) | Maintenance |
| Fill in holes in wall in library | Maintenance |
| Repair exhaust fan in Room 5 | Maintenance |
| U.S. flag and holder for cafeteria | Dick |
| Work with city on new water meter vault by plaza | Dick |
| Repair trash compacter | Maintenance |
| Large video screens installed in cafeteria/elem gym | Maintenance |
| Eliminate clutter in classrooms | Dick |
| Clean up stage area | Dick |
| Install lip in entrances to elementary shower stalls | Maintenance |
| Take down cover over north side gym windows | Maintenance |
| Heater for shop classroom | Bob |
| Repair and replace heat exchangers in North Hall and high school hall | Bob |
| Mailboxes in front of plaza | Mark |
| Art room and Spanish room modifications | Tom |
| Cabinet doors for new classrooms | Tom |
| Window replacements | Tom |
| Plaza project | Tom/George |
| Gymnasium sound baffles | Tom |
| Parking area modifications | John/Gregg |
| Elementary gym sound system | Dick |
| Privacy panels | Tom |
| Softfall for playground | John/Gregg/Loyal |
| Downtown outdoor sign | George |
| High school locker room vents | Bob |
| Repair fence by swimming pool, dugouts, shop | Maintenance |
| Order and install new slide for playground equipment | Dick |
| New gate for North Hall | Dick |
| Repair door on garage in vehicle lot | Maintenance |
| | |
| Electrical: | |
| Repair lights in north crawl space/stage | Loyal |
| Fix light fixtures in custodial closet | Loyal |
| Replace exterior light on top of cafeteria | Loyal |
| Wire new scoreboards | Loyal |
| Get electricity to outside juice machine | Loyal |
| Repair electric heaters in main shop | Loyal |

**Table 4.1.   Immediate Repair List (continued)**

| | |
|---|---|
| Repair exhaust fan in Room 5 | Loyal |
| Repair trash compactor | Loyal |
| | |
| Locks & Doors: | |
| New lock for doors between high school locker rooms | Maintenance |
| Door closure on stage door | Maintenance |
| Panic hardware for high school gym door | Maintenance |
| East cafeteria door won't lock | Maintenance |
| Replace lock on custodial door | Maintenance |
| Get door and lock system working on outside stage door | Maintenance |
| | |
| Plumbing: | |
| Fix drain in Room 1 | Maintenance |
| Connect hot water heater in Room 5 | Maintenance |
| Fix leaky faucet in shop | Maintenance |
| Turn down thermostat on hot water in shop | Maintenance |
| Repair drinking fountain in shop | Maintenance |
| Repair drinking fountain in girls' locker room | Maintenance |
| Install refrigerated drinking fountain | Maintenance |
| Water softener for boiler | Maintenance |
| | |
| Other Items/Maintenance-Custodial: | |
| Put together new teacher desks | |
| Put together new chairs | |
| Install TV and video brackets on classroom walls | |
| Assemble new butcher paper racks | |
| Build brackets for ladders | |
| Repair snow blower | |
| Repair locks on front door of high school | |
| Assemble ball carts | |
| Repair icemaker on stage | |
| Clean roof drains | |
| Remove partition wall on stage | |
| Install water filter on air lines for compressor in shop | |
| Replace two sink faucets in Room 1 | |
| Replace one sink faucet in Room 5 | |
| Replace steam pipe in high school girls' locker room | |

## Secretaries

The Walla Walla School District struggled with the need for more secretarial support at its school sites, particularly during peak times. As paperwork and reporting demands increased, state funding was decreasing.

Often, staffing formulas and allocations are built based upon high-demand periods and while there is a desire to provide the necessary level of support to handle those peak times, a district cannot always afford the salary and benefits attached to full-time positions.

In this case, the schools were provided with a bank of hours. Most of the schools found a willing parent who appreciated the possibility of part-time work. Each school could use its hours as it chose but, as might be expected, some consistent patterns emerged. The schools were provided with about 200 hours each (compared with 2,080 hours for a 12-month secretary and about 1,600 hours for someone who primarily serves during the regular school year).

For the most part, the schools used the bulk of their hours just before the start of school and as classes got underway. They also used some of their time at the end. Other uses included medical screenings, reporting periods, and similar activities that expand clerical demands.

The district was able to address special staffing needs without the added costs of benefits, leaves, and similar expenses that come with full-time employees.

## Contracting for Specialized Services

Some districts are going together to issue a call for bids for expensive, specialized services that they use from time to time. On occasion, the bids are being issued on behalf of the districts by regional service agencies or purchasing cooperatives.

Some of the most common are electrical contractors and plumbing services. By issuing an RFP (request for proposal), these consortiums or cooperatives can specify certain terms such as rate of response, licensing, quality of work, and so forth. The firms in turn quote a set rate for the local districts.

Districts have found that they can save about 25–35 percent on an hourly basis by using this method.

## Travel

One of the first things that gets dropped from a district budget is travel and, yet with a little creativity, districts can provide travel experiences at a reduced cost. Some examples might include:

- Have staff members get on the conference committee—often complimentary rooms are provided to key members of that group.

- Find accommodations near supermarkets where free samples can often be substituted for meals.
- Speaking of meals, make sure that staff members attend as many social hours as possible when attending conventions—particularly those that offer heavy hors d'oeuvres.
- Make friends with people from other districts who might be going to the same destination. Riding with them saves money.
- At the summer Confederation of Oregon School Administrators Convention in Seaside, several budding principals noted that they could find coffee and donuts every morning in the Vendor Fair. The conference draws a large number of exhibitors who set up booths and offer various enticements to lure attendees. There was also fresh popcorn and soft drinks throughout the day plus numerous candy dishes. There was a president's reception the first night with heavy hors d'oeuvres—certainly enough to suffice for dinner. The second night there were a myriad of social hours—again with more than enough food to replace dinner. This was even followed by a Dessert Fair. The young principals noted that their expenses for meals were practically nil.

On a somewhat more serious note:

- School districts, particularly those located away from metropolitan areas, often find themselves sending administrators, board members, and staff to the same location on repeated occasions. In the case of one ESD, they contacted a number of motels serving the state capitol and were able to bulk-purchase a block of 100 rooms per year at a much-reduced price. The bulk rate was $59 per night compared with a regular rate of $99 to $129. On a similar note, the ESD also has contracts at various locations around eastern Oregon and has developed a similar relationship with several other motels that are happy to have the secure revenue during what, for them, are generally off-periods.
- In the Pasco School District, where staff were often required to fly to Seattle, the district would purchase low-fare tickets ten at a time. Since September 11, that effort has become somewhat more complex.
- Encourage staff to use per diem rather than straight reimbursements for meals. The $30 per day—no questions asked—can actually pro-

duce savings. Staff members can rely on their own personal preferences for dining and have an incentive for saving money. With the straight reimbursement method—particularly considering the high costs of meals in larger venues—the costs for eating three times a day will generally exceed $30.

* When groups of staff members are going to the same location, reward car pooling. Some agencies have been fairly generous in terms of permitting staff members to take their own vehicles as a matter of personal convenience. They can still take their own car if they choose, but the obligation for the cost ought not to fall on the district. Mileage costs can add up quickly.

Some districts that used to maintain a fleet of cars, are finding that the use of rental cars can sometimes be more cost effective than having the entity actually own its own vehicles.

# 5

## Cost Savings for Community Colleges

### COMMUNITY COLLEGE ADMINISTRATION

For several years, community college administrators in Oregon have found it necessary to take steps toward reducing costs. Cost-cutting has tended to occur in a pattern, beginning with searches for new sources of income and increased productivity to meet revenue shortfalls. When such steps have not been sufficient, expenditures have been deferred, and then services have been reduced. When all of this has proved inadequate, dramatic reductions in services have been required, especially when state and local economic conditions worsen, like they are at the present time.

The following cost-saving measures indicate the variety of ideas that have been tested or are being considered on the community college campuses.

#### Increased Revenue, Productivity, or Efficiency

*New Sources of Revenue*

1. Charge laboratory fees for computer programming and other courses usually not considered lab courses.
2. Establish fees for catalogs, transcripts, job search workshops, and parking.
3. Pursue private tax-deductible donations to a foundation you set up for such purposes as endowed chairs, new facilities, and scholarships.

4. Open an electronic games center on campus, committing profits to intercollegiate athletics.
5. Eliminate third-party food services arrangements, opting to run the service with district employees or to use vending machines exclusively.
6. Revoke senior citizens' tuition waiver policy.

## Productivity and Efficiency Efforts

1. Combine small departments; eliminate some department head positions; place greater responsibility on associate deans for direct supervision.
2. Share employees with other agencies, such as school districts and city and county governments.
3. Disconnect and reduce the number of telephone lines on campus.
4. Consider a private telephone system, independent of some of larger carriers.
5. Contract for bookstore operations, custodial services, groundskeeping, and other services if cost savings can be effected.
6. Utilize volunteers for tutoring, grading papers, and other services.
7. Improve accident prevention efforts to reduce state accident insurance fund (SAIF) premiums.
8. Utilize criminal justice students as security guards for the campus.
9. Review and analyze forms used on campus, eliminating some, consolidating others.
10. Encourage energy conservation:

    • Initiate an intensive weatherization program for doors and windows.
    • Reevaluate lighting in all buildings: remove some night lights and reduce lighting where light of reading intensity is not needed.
    • Investigate the feasibility of installing a computer-assisted energy management system.
    • Place solar panels on building roofs to supplement space heating and hot water production.
    • Monitor temperature in facilities, seeking energy savings where possible.

- Change outside campus parking lights to high-presence sodium.
- "Last one out, please turn out the lights!" signs above all light switches.

## Deferred and/or Reduced Expenditures

1. Place a freeze on all out-of-state travel and reduce out-of-district travel dramatically.
2. Avoid hiring a replacement for personnel on sabbatical leave.
3. Close the campus on Friday and Saturday during summer term.
4. Place a freeze or strict review process on hiring employees to replace those leaving the institution.
5. Utilize staff development and training to prepare current employees to accept new or added responsibilities.
6. Offer early retirement packages for faculty, administrators, and classified staff only if you hire back at a lower rate of pay than those leaving.
7. Postpone solar energy efforts, thus avoiding start-up costs that have a slow payback rate.
8. Defer replacement of aging equipment, frayed drapes, worn carpets, and so forth.

## Reduced Services across-the-Board

1. Arrange for all staff members (administrative, classified, support, etc.) to take one unpaid day of leave per month as agreed with immediate supervisor.
2. Reduce the contracts for administrators, instructors, and classified staff by ten working days per fiscal year.
3. Require that the summer months of all twelve-month appointments be completed with reduced hours.
4. Consider a four-day class schedule and workweek during the academic year.
5. Close the campus for one or two weeks between summer session and fall term, and furlough staff.

**Elimination or Dramatic Reduction of Programs or Functions**

1. Streamline the organization by eliminating one or more deanships.
2. Eliminate full-time faculty positions in areas of low enrollment, such as foreign languages, music.
3. Implement a reduction-in-force plan derived through a zero-based budgeting process.
4. Freeze or restrict the hiring of part-time instructional staff, thus reducing course offerings in developmental education, adult self-improvement, and other areas.
5. Limit summer school facilities and offerings to one campus.
6. Eliminate summer session entirely.

## CURRICULUM AND INSTRUCTION

Many options are being considered by Oregon's community college districts to maintain the quality and flexibility for which they are known while they also respond to financial crises. Some of the options are described here.

**Curriculum**

1. Provide ongoing review of course offerings to determine their viability for: programs, community needs, course needs, course enrollments, comparative cost effectiveness, budgetary considerations, and so forth.
2. Offer some transfer courses on an alternate year basis.
3. Increase average class size: (1) offer some classes less often during the year, (2) cancel small classes quickly and refer students to other classes, and (3) change program requirements with fewer choices to students.
4. Give instructors the option to teach fewer students for less pay, down to a predetermined minimum.
5. Shorten fall and winter terms to eight weeks, and spring term to six weeks. Attendance may improve, instructors may remove any nonessentials from course work, and the programs may become stronger at less cost.

6. Contract with local school districts to operate programs with low enrollments. Costs could be shared and there would be less duplication of equipment purchases.
7. Share instructors with nearby college districts through teleconferencing. Low enrollment classes and programs can be filled at one-half the cost of instruction.
8. Eliminate instructional programs in small communities unless the number of tuition-paying students provides for full cost of offerings.
9. "Double-list" course offerings in small communities (credit/non-credit). The community education programs could handle the delivery of services, while the academic departments would be responsible for program quality.
10. Secure a volunteer community coordinator to plan schedules in small rural towns; provide the volunteer with free classes in return.
11. Close a center if an alternative nearby can provide the same service.
12. Secure charitable agency funding to offset the cost of classes of direct interest or benefit—for example, March of Dimes for childbirth preparation, teen parenting, prenatal care.
13. Contract for services with businesses and agencies to reduce costs and dependence on FTE. Offer courses, seminars, and workshops on a cost-plus basis.

## Instruction

1. Develop differentiated staffing for resource centers, such as a differentiated math resource center. The centers would allow for self-paced instruction, flexible course content and scheduling, open-entry, and low-cost instruction.
2. Assign administrators to duties in instruction or instructional support.
3. Investigate classes offered, particularly laboratory classes, to see if all levels could be taught in the same class. Some examples: (1) Drafting/Autocad classes I, II, and III, or (2) field labs of similar or closely related courses, such as silviculture and logging methods.

(The second example also has the advantage of teaching the interrelationships of courses.)

4. Carpool all field trips instead of using college vans, passing on the cost to the students. (Check on insurance and liability issues associated with this option.)
5. Utilize students to grade their own work and record the grades.
6. Use advanced students for peer tutoring.
7. Utilize volunteer tutors. Expand the tutor coordinator's role to include recruiting and training volunteer tutors for specific assignments.
8. Contact local service clubs and seek sponsorship of classes in ESL (English as a Second Language), Adult Basic Education, and similar programs.

## Media

1. Telecourses can be used to provide instruction to students in the outreach areas and will allow for additional flexibility on campus. Courses can be offered via cable, PBS, satellite, or V-Tel. Local school districts could use telecourses to augment district staff—for example, science and computer courses.
2. Organize a community college consortium for audiovisual software. This group would coordinate the purchasing, renting, and lending of audiovisual software among community colleges. The group also could join the Oregon Educational Computer Consortium.
3. Utilize computers for test review, test generation, and record keeping for telecourses. The savings in teacher time used for generating tests would be significant.
4. Increase or initiate use of computers for instruction in developmental education, as well as record keeping.
5. Freeze spending for equipment, library books, materials, supplies, and outside services.
6. Change video format, if you have not already done so, from 3/4-inch and 16mm to 1/2-inch. The 1/2-inch format is approximately 30 percent less expensive than 3/4-inch, and approximately 75 percent less expensive than 16mm.
7. Reduce the number of telephones on each campus.

## STUDENT SERVICES

The purpose of student services is to help students pursue their educational goals, through counseling, financial aid, and similar support. Community colleges have considered cost-saving ideas that may involve changes in existing methods, streamlining traditional programs or even changes in delivery of services. Some of the ideas are described here.

### Reduced Services to Students

1. Instead of mailing grades to students, have students who are in school the next term stop by admissions to pick up grade sheets. Those who wish them mailed could be asked to provide a stamped, self-addressed envelope.
2. Eliminate tuition waivers for student body officers and immediate family members of staff. If this is part of the collective bargaining agreements, contracts would have to be renegotiated.
3. Operate selected sports and activities on a club basis, funded by user fees or private organization sponsorship, thus removing them from the general fund budget. This could encourage initiative and responsibility on the part of participants.
4. Eliminate athletic competition in golf, tennis, cross-country, or similar programs. Fund the remaining program with vending machine revenue as supported by student government.
5. Eliminate talent grants. (This would reduce the enrollment of students needing such tuition assistance.)
6. Discontinue student services as a separate program, requiring that the faculty accept more responsibility in guidance and counseling.

### Restructured Student Services

1. Assign counselors to teach classes in career planning, job search, test anxiety, study skills techniques, and similar support. This could result in less one-on-one counseling.
2. Use students to help in replacing or supplementing classified positions.
3. Ask every student to donate some work time to the college, even if it is only a few hours per term for part-time students. This may not

cut custodial or maintenance costs but would help accomplish a variety of tasks.

4. Allow students to barter for waived tuition. In return for $X$ number of hours of work for the college (i.e., maintenance, clerical support, lab assistance, etc.), they could be allowed to enroll in $Y$ number of credit (or noncredit) courses at no charge.

## Streamlined Student Services

1. Consolidate use of Career Information System in a cooperative effort by ESDs, public high schools, and community colleges. This would lower the cost per institution.
2. Implement a yearlong computer-produced schedule. Students could plan their school work schedule for the academic year, but there would be less flexibility.
3. Revise office procedures so that all registration material is put in to the central computer by the field offices.
4. Computerize the student services area, including (1) online registration with associated list generation, (2) financial aid and veterans, (3) follow-up, (4) self-help advising/scheduling/career analysis. This would encourage accurate monitoring of programs, reduce staff needed for clerical/routine functions, and release professional time to perform professional functions.
5. Review other college publications through sharing arrangements concerned with registration to determine whether their formats are less costly to produce and mail.
6. Replace the annually printed and bound adviser's handbook with a three-ring binder into which a loose-leaf handbook and other documents related to academic advising are placed. Replace annually only those portions that need revision.

## EXPANDED COST-SAVING IDEAS

### Expanded Idea #1

Increase accident prevention efforts, especially in high risk areas, focusing on job safety and safety training materials. The result should be a decrease in on-the-job accidents.

*Advantages:* Fewer lost workdays; savings in annual workers' compensation insurance premium costs (one community college has realized a savings of more than $150,000 in a three-year period); may result in a better work environment for all employees and enhance employee morale. Clearly, it is important that the SAIF (state accident insurance fund) retro payment plan information be continued. Any safety program requires the continued support of staff and administration. Disadvantages could include the cost of training materials.

## Expanded Idea #2

Reduce the contracts for administrators, instructors, and classified staff by ten working days per fiscal year.

*Advantages:* Savings would be significant, yet the reduction in time would not necessarily have a drastic effect on college operations or instruction; avoids layoff of personnel.

*Disadvantages:* All staff would receive ten (10) days less pay.

*Additional Information:* The cooperation of both the classified and professional unions would be helpful in implementing this plan, or else the board would need to declare a financial emergency.

## Expanded Idea #3

Allow students to barter for waived tuition. In return for $X$ number of hours of work for the college (e.g., maintenance, clerical support, laboratory assistant), they could be allowed to enroll in $Y$ number of credit (or noncredit) courses at no charge.

*Advantages:* Classes would be available to students otherwise unable to afford the instruction. Maintenance of buildings would be accomplished, perhaps at less cost. Work experience would be gained by students who might otherwise have none. Students would take more pride in their college by being an active part of it.

*Disadvantages:* Administrative time would be needed to establish and monitor the program. Safeguards against poor performance would be needed. Forms would need to be developed and the business office would need tuition waiver procedures.

*Additional Information:* Probably one full-time employee's time would be needed to approve bartering plans, monitor performance of the agreed-upon tasks, and arrange tuition-free enrollment. Tasks that would qualify for the barter system would have to be clearly defined and procedures developed. It would probably be most effective if students worked prior to enrollment in class to build up the "work credit." This would eliminate problems with noncompletion of the barter agreement.

## Expanded Idea #4

Replace the annually printed and bound adviser's handbook with a three-ring binder into which a loose-leaf handbook and other documents related to academic advising are placed. Replace annually only those portions that need revision.

*Advantages:* Reduced staff time in preparing copy for the handbook with only an initial outlay of money, time, and energy; reduced cost of printing and binding; easier and faster updating of handbook contents; more flexibility for revisions as they occur, rather than once each year; advising materials are included in a single binder.

*Disadvantages:* Initial cost for three-ring binders; preparation of the full set the first time is time-consuming; binders are larger and potentially less convenient to use.

# 6

## Generating Alternative
## Revenue Sources in Education

According to De Luna (1998), "The hottest fund-raising trend in public education is local education foundations (LEFs). With today's revenue shortfalls, educators and parents are seeking assistance from private sources. Locally funded and operated foundations separate from the local school district emerged during the property-tax limitations measures passed in the 1980s in such states as California, Oregon, and Massachusetts."

There are about 2,000 LEFs throughout the nation, according to De Luna (1998). Merz and Frankel (1997) found that the average amount raised by most school foundations is only about .3 percent of a typical district's budget. LEFs employ many fund-raising techniques, such as direct solicitation letter campaigns, use of special credit cards, dinners, golf tournaments, car raffles, and auctions (De Luna 1998).

LEFs are nonprofit, tax-exempt third parties that foster educational innovation and school improvement and help fill the gap while supplying schools and districts with needed funds, equipment, and services donated by generous alumni, community members, and businesses who are able to take a tax deduction.

LEFs with strong financial bases are rare. According to Merz and Frankel's national study, LEFs that raise $10,000 or less annually usually provide minigrants to staff and scholarships to students; those that collect from $20,000 to $50,000 usually fund curriculum enrichment programs; and those that raise $100,000 or more often underwrite special teaching positions (Merz and Frankel 1997; De Luna 1998).

In addition to utilizing LEFs, many districts are also pursuing other very creative fund-raising strategies, such as partnerships with booster clubs and businesses; programs for soliciting volunteers or businesses for in-kind donations utilizing tax deductible receipts; selling and leasing services and facilities; generating income from student-run businesses; generating investment income; collecting pay-to-play fees to fund sports and cocurricular activities; holding and sponsoring schoolwide fund-raising events such as bottle and can drives; cooperating with social-services providers through bill-back programs to Medicaid; partnerships or interagency agreements with park and recreation districts to fund certain programs, allowing the school district to free up funds currently being used on these activities to be used for other high-priority school programs and services; and pursuing government and private foundation grants (Pijanowski and Monk 1996; Monk and Brent 1997).

Other fund-raising strategies have included ideas like the following: becoming the area's Internet service provider, renting out buses and drivers to community groups and forest firefighters, organizing for-profit fish farms and agricultural farmers run by students, and school retail stores such as a hardware and farm feed and seed run out of the vocational department, which gets materials and supplies at wholesale and sells them at retail.

More controversial fund-raisers used in some districts include agreements with businesses for allowing advertising on school property. Molnar and Morales (2000) estimate that between 1990 and 2000, commercial activities in schools have multiplied several times over in areas such as:

- Fund-raising
- Privatization of school programs and services
- Electronic marketing
- Corporate-sponsored educational materials
- Sponsorship of programs and activities
- Exclusive agreements with corporations
- Incentive programs
- Appropriation of space
- Corporate matching programs
- Grocery script and soup-label campaigns
- Discount rebates back to schools for referring shoppers to a store

States have also generated new revenue sources not dependent solely on property taxes, such as funds for schools from state-run lotteries and funds from lawsuit settlements with top tobacco companies (Garret 2001; Manzo 2000).

## CASE STUDY EXAMPLE: PERRYDALE SCHOOL DISTRICT NO. 21, PERRYDALE, OREGON

Strategic plans for generating alternative sources of revenue must be designed to fit the unique needs of the district you are serving at the time. For example, the Perrydale School District No. 21 in Perrydale, Oregon, under the direction of Tim Adsit, developed the following strategic plan that was successful in increasing district revenues by over $860,000, cutting costs by over $60,000, and placing the district in a more stable financial position after tax limitations had almost caused it to declare bankruptcy:

- Focus the district on the mission of continually improving student learning, achievement, and excellence;
- Lobby local legislators to draft new legislation to increase school funding without increasing property taxes;
- Establish an education foundation;
- Implement a four-days-per-week class schedule;
- Conduct a cost reduction study and implement the good ideas generated;
- Write grants;
- Expand the district's student population (which works well in states that have average daily membership weighted formulas (admw) for funding basic school support);
- Restructure schooling to expand the curriculum without expanding the staff by implementing distance learning and computer instruction technologies;
- Establish school/business partnerships that raise revenues or increase resources and that are mutually beneficial to the district and the business partner;
- Share costs and services with various districts and agencies, including parks and recreation districts, through consortiums and develop-

ing interagency agreements to provide personnel and services at the school site in exchange for use of school facilities when not in use by school students or personnel;

• Plan, develop, and implement various entrepreneurial enterprises and student-run businesses that help to pay for some or all of the class and student-run business; and

• Stay in a continuous process of school improvement, strategic planning, and change, focused on your mission and on increasing revenues and reducing costs.

## SAMPLE OF STRATEGIC PLANS AND CREATIVE IDEAS FOR GENERATING ALTERNATIVE REVENUES

### Crane Elementary and High School Districts

In addition, sample strategic plans for generating alternative revenues, developed while Tim Adsit was serving as the superintendent of schools in Crane Union High School District No. 1J and Crane Elementary School District No. 4, include the following:

Adopted Strategic Plan to Generate Alternative Sources of Revenue for Crane Union High School District No. 1J

1. Total commitment to excellence through increased efficiency, accountability, service, employee training, increased parent involvement, and service to gain higher student achievement and mastery of the new basics for the 21st Century.

2. Lobby our legislators at both the State and Federal level for new funds. For example, county roads funds must now be used as an offset against State School Fund revenue support. Encourage our federal legislators to get this bill changed at the federal level so these funds can be used in addition to State school support. Continue lobbying our legislators in regards to many forms of legislation that will either increase revenue or assist in cutting expenses in our schools.

3. Establish a Crane Area Schools Education Foundation, which will allow people and businesses to donate money, goods, or services and receive tax write-offs for doing so. Private funds raised by this Foundation could be used to help offset revenue losses from public funds and help

us preserve excellence in Crane Education. The Boards in both districts have already implemented this proposal.

4. Conduct a study and implement agreed upon recommendations for cost savings that are feasible. The staffs in both districts have already implemented this proposal.

5. Write grants to attract alternative revenue sources. Such grants can either be written by the district, the foundation or both.

6. Utilize all appropriate forms of technology to deliver instruction in different ways. Restructure schooling and the delivery of instructional services, as we currently know them through full utilization of technology and full implementation of Oregon's Education Action for the 21st Century. Not only maintain our current accreditation status with the State and with the Northwest Association of Schools and Colleges, but also become a model 21st Century School Site that receives local, state, national and international recognition.

Establish school-business partnerships and entrepreneurial enterprises both on and off the school site that generate income and job sites for Crane students in grades 7–12. Use some of the profit generated by these programs to help fund the operational expenses of the program.

8. Share costs and services with local area districts, the ESD, a consortium of districts, county and state agencies, the business sector and higher education while still maintaining Crane Union High School District's identity and autonomy.

9. Conduct further study and gain public input on the concept of voting to develop a small parks and recreation district for the full funding of such high school programs as arts, crafts, and woodshop, music, outdoor education, interscholastic athletics, performing arts, vocational agriculture, and home economics.

Such a recreation district is capable of utilizing the boundaries of the CUHS District for taxing itself anywhere from $0 up to $10.00 per thousand of assessed valuation. Parks and recreation districts were not limited to $5.00/1000 of assessed valuation under Measure 5, which passed a number of years ago like schools were.

This newly formed parks and recreation district would have its own Board of Directors and any employees and programs offered by the newly formed district would be paid from the new district's budget and not from the school district's general fund budget. Another way to accomplish this would be for the newly formed parks and recreation district to enter into an interagency agreement with the CUHS District to pay for these services with the programs and employee's staying at the school. This is the method used in Morrow County School District, Morrow County, Oregon, for example.

Basically, the formation of such a parks and recreation district would give local taxpayers a way around the limitations of Measure 5 and it would restore some degree of local control to district taxpayers who are looking for new sources of revenues to support schools. This idea still uses increased public tax dollars, but it is a better idea than voting a local school levy in addition to state revenues anticipated to be received, because those revenues have to be used as an offset against school support at the present time unless the law is changed. On the other hand, the revenues generated by the newly formed parks and recreation district are in addition to the school district's current level of funding.

This proposal would have to go before the Harney County Commissioners who would have to vote to allow such a proposal to be on the ballot using the boundaries of CUHS District as the boundaries for the newly formed parks and recreation district.

Give the matter some thought, it has great possibilities for resolving most of the current school revenue problems.

10. Continue to add other ideas for generating alternative revenues not solely dependent on property taxes. Implement these new ideas as the Board, staff, administration, parents, students and public are able to reach consensus on them. Brainstorm now to generate more quality ideas!

Adopted Strategic Plan to Generate Alternative Sources of Revenue Crane Elementary School District No. 4

1. Total commitment to excellence through increased efficiency, accountability, service, employee training, increased parent involvement, and service to gain higher student achievement and mastery of the new basics for the 21st Century.
2. Lobby our legislators at both the State and Federal level for new funds. For example, county roads funds must now be used as an offset against State School Fund revenue support. Encourage our federal legislators to get this bill changed at the federal level so these funds can be used in addition to State school support. Continue lobbying our legislators in regards [sic] to many forms of legislation that will either increase revenue or assist in cutting expenses in our schools.
3. Establish a Crane Area Schools Education Foundation, which will allow people and businesses to donate money, goods, or services and

receive tax write-offs for doing so. Private funds raised by this Foundation could be used to help offset revenue losses from public funds and help us preserve excellence in Crane Education. The Boards in both districts have already implemented this proposal.

4. Conduct a study and implement agreed upon recommendations for cost savings that are feasible. The staffs in both districts have already implemented this proposal.

5. Write grants to attract alternative revenue sources. Such grants can either be written by the district, the foundation or both.

6. Utilize all appropriate forms of technology to deliver instruction in different ways. Restructure schooling and the delivery of instructional services, as we currently know them through full utilization of technology and full implementation of Oregon's Education Action for the 21st Century. Not only maintain our current accreditation status with the State and with the Northwest Association of Schools and Colleges, but also become a model 21st Century School Site that receives local, state, national and international recognition.

7. Establish school-business partnerships and entrepreneurial enterprises both on and off the school site that generate income and job sites for Crane students in grades 7–12. Use some of the profit generated by these programs to help fund the operational expenses of the program.

8. Share costs and services with local area districts, the ESD, a consortium of districts, county and state agencies, the business sector and higher education while still maintaining Crane Elementary School District's identity and autonomy.

9. Continue to add other ideas for generating alternative revenues not solely dependent on property taxes. Implement these new ideas as the Board, staff, administration, parents, students and public are able to reach consensus on them. Brainstorm now to generate more quality ideas!

Another strategic planning idea for generating revenues and cutting costs is the concept of "value engineering." Once your strategic plan is in order, enter into the value engineering process whereby other experts literally "second-guess" the plan or project. This process invariably leads to huge savings and introduces valuable alternatives and considerations. School districts would be well advised to bring in experts from time to time for a modest fee to second-guess how they are spending their money and make objective suggestions. It is almost guaranteed that the savings will outstrip the costs by a wide margin.

Also, we are at a time when local and/or superintendent control is a thing of the past. We need to find every conceivable partner who will do something for us that will save money and expand service. Schools have not been the most welcoming of places for people who wish to share their thoughts and ideas, whether we admit it or not. Educators like to think of themselves as the local experts. We need to shed that mantle and consider every conceivable idea and suggestion that helps make us more effective and efficient.

As we stated earlier, we don't have as much of a lack of a money problem in public education as we have a lack of creative ideas problem. As educators we must learn to think outside the box and change our paradigms.

# 7

## A Very Brief Summary

Districts will vary in the extent of their financial problems and in the solutions they apply to those problems; for some, it will be "business as usual," others will need to cut staff and programs. The ideas presented in this book are intended to cover a broad range of possibilities, and any number of planning approaches may be needed. There are no prepackaged answers. However, from personal experience with implementing many of the cost-saving ideas presented in this book during our combined years of service in school administration to date, we can tell you that the process is a creative one and you will generate many other useful ideas unique to solving your district's problems simply from reviewing the ideas presented.

We hope you will make this book a work in progress and share your ideas with us for inclusion in a planned sequel to this book based upon ideas that are shared from readers across the world. At the back of this book, you'll find a form to submit your own creative ideas for cutting costs and generating revenues. You may reach us at the following address and phone number:

Tim Adsit,
POB 861
Crane, OR 97732
Phone: 1-541-493-2361
e-mail: timads@centurytel.net.

The Chinese symbol for crisis is a combination of the characters *danger* and *opportunity*. While cutting budgets is difficult and often painful, in a very strong sense it also presents an opportunity for new approaches to thinking, and it can serve as a catalyst for drawing the community and school together. Finding the balance between expedient short-term remedies and long-term solutions places great demands on the creativity and leadership abilities of all involved.

An equal amount of time should also be given to strategically planning, developing, and implementing creative ideas that will generate alternative revenue sources not dependent solely on property taxes for operating our public schools.

# Appendix A

## AEPA School Purchasing Cooperative Members

### ARIZONA

Mohave Educational Services Cooperative
625 East Beale Street
Kingman, AZ 86401
www.mesc.org

Jim Migliorino
Executive Director
5225 N. Central Avenue, Ste. 218
Phoenix, AZ 85012
Phone: 602-277-4290
Fax: 602-277-4286
E-mail: jim@mesc.org

Tom Peeler
Purchasing Director
625 East Beale Street
Kingman, AZ 86401
Phone: 928-753-6945
Fax: 928-718-3233
E-mail: tom@mesc.org

### CALIFORNIA

Monterey County Office of Education
www.calsave.org

Mike Mellon
CalSAVE and AEPA Project
    Director
c/o Monterey County Office
    of Education
901 Blanco Circle
POB 80851
Salinas, CA 93912
Phone: 831-755-0383
Fax: 831-784-4167
E-mail:
mmellon@monterey.k12.ca.us

Dave Finley
CalSAVE and AEPA Project
    Manager
c/o Monterey County Office
    of Education
901 Blanco Circle
POB 80851
Salinas, CA 93912
Phone: 831-755-6495
Fax: 831-784-4167
E-mail:
dfinley@monterey.k12.ca.us

## COLORADO

Colorado BOCES Association
E-mail: jtillman@slvbocs.org
Web address: www.slvbocs.org

John Tillman
Colorado BOCES Representative
c/o San Luis Valley BOCES
Box 119
Alamosa, CO 81101
Phone: 719-589-5851
Fax: 719-589-5007

David R. Thompson
President
c/o Pikes Peak BOCES
4825 Lorna Pl.
Colorado Springs, CO 80915
Phone: 719-570-7474
Fax: 719-380-9685
E-mail: dthompson@ppboces.org
Web address: www.ppboces.org

## INDIANA

Wilson Education Center
www.wesc.k12.in.us

Larry E. Risk
Executive Director
11440 Highway 62
Charlestown, IN 47111-9400
Phone: 812-256-8000
Fax: 812-256-8012
E-mail: lerisk@wesc.k12.in.us

Pam Clover
Director of Business
11440 Highway 62
Charlestown, IN 47111-9400
Phone: 812-256-8000
Fax: 812-256-8012
E-mail: pclover@wesc.k12.in.us

## IOWA

Iowa Educators Consortium
www.iec-ia.org

Dan Dreyer
Director
3712 Cedar Heights Drive
Cedar Falls, IA 50613
Phone: 319-273-8211
Fax: 319-273-8229
E-mail: ddreyer@aea267.k12.ia.us

Jerry Cochrane
Media and Technology Coordinator
4401 6th Street SW
Cedar Rapids, IA 52404
Phone: 319-399-6700
Fax: 319-399-6457
E-mail: jcochrane@aea10.k12.ia.us

## KANSAS

Southeast Kansas Education Service Center
www.greenbush.org

Steve Spade
Purchasing
POB 189-947 West 57 Hwy
Girard, KS 66743-0189
Phone: 620-724-6281
Fax: 620-724-6284
E-mail: steve.spade@greenbush.org

Cinda Holmes
Cooperative Purchasing Coordinator
POB 189-947 West 57 Hwy
Girard, KS 66743-0189
Phone: 620-724-6281
Fax: 620-724-6284
E-mail:
cinda.holmes@greenbush.org

## KENTUCKY

Green River Regional Educational Cooperative
www.grrec.coop.k12.ky.us

Liz Storey
Executive Director
Green River Regional Educational
Cooperative
Western Kentucky University
427 Tate-Page Hall
Bowling Green, KY 42101-3576
Phone: 270-745-2451
Fax: 270-745-5199
E-mail:
lstorey@grrec.coop.k12.ky.su

Ann Burden
Bids Coordinator
Green River Regional Educational
Cooperative
Western Kentucky University
427 Tate-Page Hall
Bowling Green, KY 42101-3576
Phone: 270-745-2451
Fax: 270-745-5199
E-mail:
aburden@grre.coop.k12.ky.us

## MINNESOTA

North Central Service Cooperative
www.ncscmn.org

Mike Hajek
Director of Business Development
and Marketing
200 1st Street NE
Staples, MN 56479-9502
Phone: 218-894-5477
Fax: 218-894-3045
E-mail: mike@ncscnm.org

Ken Shane
Sales Manager
200 1st Street NE
Staples, MN 56479-9502
Phone: 218-894-5490
Fax: 218-894-3045
E-mail: ken@ncscm.org

## MISSOURI

Cooperating School Districts www.schoolsupplies.org,
www.moprc.org

Tom Post
Business Department
1460 Craig Road
St. Louis, MO 63146-4842
Phone: 800-818-7486
Fax: 314-872-7970
E-mail: tom@reapmail.net

Bob Slama
Director of Business Services
1460 Craig Road
St. Louis, MO 63146-4842
Phone: 800-818-7486
Fax: 314-872-8167
E-mail: bslama@reapmail.net

## MONTANA

Montana Cooperative Service Corporation
www.mtcoop.org

Frank Loehding
Administrator Director
307 1st Street
Bainville, MT 59212
Phone: 406-769-2502
Fax: 406-765-2501
E-mail: floehd@mtcoop.org

## NEBRASKA

Nebraska ESU Cooperative Purchasing
www.esu17.k12.ne.us/~necoop

Lynn W. Thorpe
Executive Director
1292 E. 4th
Ainsworth, NE 69210
Phone: 800-584-9802
Fax: 402-387-2530
E-mail: lthorpe@esu17.org

Paul Utemark
Assistant Executive Director
1292 E. 4th
Ainsworth, NE 69210
Phone: 402-387-1245
Fax: 402-387-2530
E-mail: utemarkp@esu17.org

## NEW MEXICO

Cooperative Educational Services
www.nedu.org

Max Luft
Executive Director
4216 Balloon Park Road NE
Albuquerque, NM 87109
Phone: 505-344-5470
Fax: 505-344-9343
E-mail: mluft@nmedu.org

Llew Perry
Assistant Executive Director
4216 Balloon Park Road NE
Albuquerque, NM 87109
Phone: 505-344-5470
Fax: 505-344-9343
E-mail: lperry@nmedu.org

## NORTH DAKOTA

North Dakota Educators Service Cooperative
www.ndesc.org

John Jankowski
President
North Dakota Educators Service
   Cooperative
c/o St. Mary's Central High School
1025 North Second Street
Bismarck, ND 58501
Phone: 701-223-4113
Fax: 701-223-8629
E-mail:
john.jankowski.1@sendit.nodak.edu

Jane Eastes
Manager of Administrative Services
Cooperative Resources,
   Incorporated
1001 E. Mount Faith
Fergus Falls, MN 56537
Phone: 218-739-3273
Fax: 218-739-2459
E-mail: jeastes@lcsc.org

## OHIO

Ohio Council of Educational Purchasing Consortium
www.ocepc.org

Elmo Kallner
Executive Director
Metropolitan Educational Council
2100 City Gate Drive
Columbus, OH 43219
Phone: 614-473-8300
Fax: 614-473-8324
E-mail: kallner@mecdc.org
Web address: www.mecdc.org

Ken Swink
Executive Director
Southwestern Ohio Edu.
   Purchasing Council
1831 Harshman Road
Dayton, OH 45424-5094
Phone: 937-236-6684
Fax: 937-236-2749
E-mail: ep_director@mdeca.org
Web address: www.epc-online.org

## OREGON

Umatilla-Morrow ESD
www.umesd.k12.or.us

Tammy Standley
Cooperative Purchasing Coordinator
2001 SW Nye
Pendleton, OR 97801
Phone: 541-966-3119
Fax: 541-966-3205
E-mail:
tammy_standley@umesd.k12.or.us

## PENNSYLVANIA

Central Susquehanna Intermediate Unit #16
90 Lawton Lane
Milton, PA 17847
www.paejpc.or

Jeff Kimball
Cooperative Purchasing Services
 Mgr.
POB 213
Lewisburg, PA 17837
Phone: 570-523-1155 ext. 2130
Fax: 570-524-5600
E-mail: jkimball@csiu.org

Jim Randecker
Procurement Tech and Services
 Administrator
POB 213
Lewisburg, PA 17837
Phone: 570-523-1155 ext. 2115
Fax: 570-522-0577
E-mail: jrandecker@csiu.org

## SOUTH DAKOTA

Mid-Central Educational Cooperative
www.mid-centralcoop.org

Scott Westerhuis
Assistant Director
POB 228
612 South Main Street
Platte, SD 57369
Phone: 605-337-2636
Fax: 605-337-2271
E-mail: westersal@yahoo.com

## TEXAS

Region IV Education Service Center
7145 West Tidwell
Houston, TX 77092-2096
www.esc4.net

Stuart Verdon
Director, TCPN
7145 West Tidwell
Houston, TX 77092-2096
Phone: 713-744-8115
Fax: 713-744-6514
E-mail: sverdon@esc4.net

Pete Paul
11213 Cezanne St.
Austin, TX 78726
Phone: 512-257-0128
Cell: 512-917-9859
Fax: 713-744-6514
E-mail: petepaul@austin.rr.com

# VIRGINIA

Fairfax County Public Schools
www.fcps.edu

Tony Crosby
6800-B Industrial Road
Springfield, VA 22151
Phone: 703-658-3601
Fax: 703-642-9159
E-mail: tony.crosby@fcps.edu

# WASHINGTON

King County Directors' Association
18639 80th Avenue South
Kent, WA 98032
www.kcda.org

Jim Borrow                          Dave Uglem
Executive Director                  Purchasing Manager
POB 5550                            POB 5550
Kent, WA 98064-5550                 Kent, WA 98064-5550
Phone: 425-251-8115 ext. 161        Phone: 425-251-8115 ext. 143
Fax: 253-395-5402                   Fax: 253-395-5402
E-mail: jborrow@kcda.org            E-mail: duglem@kcda.org

# WYOMING

Northeast Wyoming Board of Cooperative Educational Services
www.new-bocs.k12.wy.us

David L. Swantek
Executive Director
410 North Miller Avenue
Gillette, Wyoming 82716
Phone: 307-682-0231
Fax: 307-686-7628
E-mail: dls@wy-net.com

# Appendix B

## Cost-cutting and Revenue Generating Ideas to Use with Staff, Advisory Groups, and Community Members[1]

*Directions and Key:* Circle the letter code that best describes your reaction to the creative idea(s) presented by chapter below.

*Key:*

P = Possibly worth investigating for use in our school district.
W = Worth investigating for use in our school district.
I = Illegal in our state at the present time.
N = Not useful, practical, or possible at the present time in our school district.
O = Other creative idea generated from reviewing this idea. Write idea down before proceeding.

### CHAPTER 1: THE PROBLEM OF DECLINING FUNDS FOR SCHOOLS AND SOLUTION STRATEGIES

P W I N O    1.1   Have you considered the skills of your staff outside the areas of their professional training? You may have access to good part-time carpenters, mechanics, and so forth, or those who could help with drama, music, athletics, and similar activities because of hobbies or other work experience.

[1] The authors have granted permission to reproduce this instrument in its entirety or by section for use with staff, advisory groups, and community members.

153

P W I N O     1.2 Have you considered exchange/trade-off arrangements with local business or industry (e.g., free lunches for volunteers to work with disabled children, businesses to provide on-site learning settings, work experience stations, or consultants in exchange for use of school facilities for their employees in the evenings, etc.)?

P W I N O     1.3 Have you considered different avenues of cooperative interagency agreements between schools, between districts, through ESDs, cities, counties, or community colleges or cooperatives for sharing resources (e.g., mechanics, repair and maintenance contracts, or for group purchase of materials, supplies, or commodities)?

P W I N O     1.4 Are you utilizing vocational education classes for construction projects such as bookcases, partitions, rebuilding, or refinishing furniture?

P W I N O     1.5 Have you fully explored all angles of parent/volunteer involvement such as garage sales, auctions, flea markets, donations, help as playground supervisors, help locating used furniture or equipment from business or government offices where they are cutting back or upgrading their existing inventory?

P W I N O     1.6 In analyzing its present and projected fiscal situation, a district may find it useful to describe the anticipated balance between income and budget needs.

P W I N O     1.7 A large number of variables determine a district's budget, many of which cannot be predicted with any degree of certainty. However, knowledge or at least estimates of the following will help clarify the financial picture beyond the immediate future:

- Future student enrollment by grade.
- Demographic, economic, and political trends at the local and state level affecting voter willingness to approve tax increases, requests for salary increases, nonpersonnel costs, and attitudes toward school closure, and school choice or homeschool initiatives.

- General economic and political trends at the state level affecting state school fund support, property tax relief, grant-in-aid programs, timber revenues, property tax limitation initiatives and measures, etc.
- Trends in the level and method of federal support for education.
- Budgets and audit reports tracking district resources and expenditures over time.

P W I N O   1.8 This process of resolving budget concerns may occur in five suggested stages: setting ground rules, parameters, and policies, involving staff and community, examining cost-cutting alternatives, presenting options to the board of directors, and evaluating the impact of budget reduction.

P W I N O   1.9 When working with district staff:

1. The superintendent should meet with union leadership as soon as practicable to explain the financial crisis. Suggest that they look at negotiated contracts to see if some changes could help reduce costs. Reassure the unions that no unilateral action is contemplated.

2. Set forth any legal, contractual, state, or federal standards compliance limitations, such as maintenance of effort regulations, that may affect budgeting. Make clear the extent to which these factors can or cannot be negotiated or waived.

3. Inform and involve all segments of the staff—building-level administrators, professional staff, support and maintenance staff, and bus drivers. Establish study groups using the ideas, coding system, prioritization processes, and group input materials found in this book to analyze suggestions, set priorities among those suggestions, draft impact statements, and make recommendations.

P W I N O   1.10 *Level 1: Increase productivity.* The district may decide to enlarge class sizes, coordinate or consolidate similar functions within the district or with other districts (in such areas as purchasing, transportation, or media programs), use computer-assisted instruction, two-way, interactive video, Internet courses, satellite TV, correspondence, or other distance-learning technologies to meet certain instructional needs, economize (on supplies, electricity, etc.), or in other ways bring about greater cost effectiveness.

P W I N O  1.11 *Level 2: Defer spending.* The district may "make do" for the time being on such matters as maintenance, capital outlay, or textbook purchases. These decisions must be made with care, to avoid expenses in the future that would be unnecessary if sound preventative measures were to be taken now.

P W I N O  1.12 *Level 3: Reduce services by cutting program budgets equally.* "Across the board" reductions in spending might be sufficient to solve the budget problems; each program administrator would be required to find a way to cut back a given percentage — somewhere. By spreading relatively small cuts across the entire organization, nearly the same level of quality can be maintained.

P W I N O  1.13 *Level 4: Eliminate nonessential services.* Rather than force deeper cuts across all programs, a district may decide to do without certain programs or services altogether. Certain athletic programs, staff support services, school food service, student transportation, and so forth might fall into this category.

P W I N O  1.14 *Level 5: Eliminate or drastically reduce positions, programs, and services.* After most other options have been exhausted, professional staff reduction remains as a last resort. Options to consider include voluntary agreement to take unpaid furloughs, early retirement, reducing the workweek to four days, eliminating staff positions, or in some other way trimming salary costs. Other severe alternatives are consolidation with another district, school closure, and instructional program elimination.

P W I N O  1.15 Other factors being equal, those programs that can be rebuilt more easily without sacrificing quality might be cut first; those that would take years to reestablish might be protected.

P W I N O  1.16 If a district expects deficits over the next two or three years, budget cuts beyond those needed to balance the coming year's budget should be analyzed. In this manner, for example, if reduction-in-force is decided upon, savings might be compounded over three years rather than one by making this difficult decision now.

P W I N O     1.17 "Cutback impact statements" can help to organize information, including opinions and perceptions, about the consequences of a given reduction, showing clearly what is being sacrificed.

An impact statement might include:
- A general description of the cutback proposal;
- The number of students involved and how they are affected;
- The number of staff involved and how they are affected;
- The consequences (advantages and disadvantages);
- Possible effect on other programs or services;
- Legal implications (e.g., regarding state standards, handicapped laws, etc.); and
- Dollars saved.

P W I N O     1.18 *Priorities.* Setting priorities lies at the heart of the matter in adjusting school budgets. Establish processes for identifying and rank-ordering priorities.

P W I N O     1.19 *Evaluating the Impact of Budget Reduction.* The study of changes in program effectiveness and productivity following budget cuts will provide useful information for future budget decisions. Districts may wish to share ideas, data collection instruments and processes, sample evaluation studies and templates for presenting data to the school board, staff, local community members, legislators, and tips on using evaluation data in the budgeting process.

## CHAPTER 2: COST-SAVING TIPS FOR DISTRICT AND SCHOOL-LEVEL ADMINISTRATION

### District Administration

P W I N O     2.1 Recover more of the direct costs for such programs as school lunch, interschool activities, special electives, adult education, and evening activities.

P W I N O 2.2 Extend the school day and reduce the week to four or four and one-half days. (No substitutes for coaches.)

P W I N O 2.3 Reduce the number of administrators through multiassignment.

P W I N O 2.4 Organize schedules so that specialized staff can work in two or more buildings.

P W I N O 2.5 Develop a well-planned reduction-in-force policy, which will allow for the transfer of staff to improve pupil-teacher ratios in specialized areas.

P W I N O 2.6 In larger districts with multiple schools, consider closing school buildings not needed. Research, develop criteria, establish procedures for closure, strategically plan for the management of conflict and political backlash that comes with school closure in many cases.

**Business**

P W I N O 2.7 *Contracting Services.* Responsibility for building and grounds maintenance, food service operations, transportation, custodial services, insurance, computer applications and technology support, and so forth can be considered for private contracting, or obtained through education service districts.
- Prepare bidding specifications carefully.
- Prepare cost studies for use in making cost comparisons.
- Termination clauses provide protection from poor service or loss in financial support as a result of levy failures, or federal/state revenue reductions.
- The district's labor agreements must allow for such contracting.

P W I N O 2.8 *Insurance.* Money often can be saved by bidding for insurance, and almost all types of insurance can be bid successfully.
- Prepared specifications are key to successful bidding.
- Consultants can help reduce risks, losses, and costs.
- Be sure that insurance possibilities are not restricted by employee bargaining agreements.

• Local agents and firms should not be given preference.
• Some districts (or a consortium) may consider self-insurance.

P W I N O  2.9 *Computers.* Computerization of business services can cut costs and increase efficiency if implemented correctly.
• Computers for business can be used to some degree by districts of any size.
• Many good business software packages complete with tech support services are available to most districts at reasonable costs.
• Beware of software limitations and how the particular software you are considering meshes with state and federal reporting requirements and forms to be submitted electronically before buying or leasing any data processing hardware.
• The computer programs developed by some districts for scheduling transportation maintenance have improved cost effectiveness.

P W I N O  2.10 Improve the management of cash flow from all sources.
• Lower the number of "idle fund" days.
• Increase cash flow monitoring (minicomputers, charts).
• Improve investment policies and practices.
• Demand district money held by the county.

P W I N O  2.11 Increase cooperative business functions; decrease the number of staff working on business functions. Watch for duplicate accounting systems in district programs.

P W I N O  2.12 Expand the use of regional purchasing for supplies, equipment, and vehicles.
• Use disposable items (mops, filters, etc.)

P W I N O  2.13 Establish a multiyear capital improvement plan.
• What can be put off now?
• What will the costs be later if the scheduled protective maintenance or project is put off now?

P W I N O  2.14 Look to the various business task force on education recommendations available from your state's local lobbying group for business as a resource.

P W I N O    2.15 The Public Contract Review Board rules in your state apply to the sale of public property just as they do to purchasing. As an example, in Oregon, for any item valued at $500 or more, a district must try to obtain three quotes; on items less than $500, quotes are encouraged.

## Personnel

*Ideas That Increase Revenue, Productivity, or Efficiency*

P W I N O    2.16 Utilize staff development and training to prepare current employees for new or added responsibilities.
  • Train district staff to serve in staff development roles.
  • Train teachers for new positions by providing in-service, graduate course reimbursement, and so forth.

P W I N O    2.17 Invite bargaining units to participate in cost cutting through "quality circles"—small groups of employees who meet to discuss work and identify ways to become more productive.

P W I N O    2.18 Develop a well-planned reduction-in-force policy whereby staff members can be transferred to improve pupil-teacher ratios in specialized areas.

P W I N O    2.19 Stagger building schedules so that specialized staff can work in two or more buildings and students can be transported more efficiently.

P W I N O    2.20 Combine two or more part-time positions into one full-time position.

P W I N O    2.21 When an additional class section is needed in a secondary school, pay a regular teacher to work an extra period rather than hiring a teacher for that period.

P W I N O    2.22 Hire two or three "permanent substitutes" to replace absent staff members. This may provide for better substitute service.

P W I N O    2.23 Place all administrators on eight-hour day, twelve-month contracts.

P W I N O    2.24 Extend the working day for consultants.

P W I N O    2.25 Redescribe staff responsibilities.
- Analyze job descriptions for cooks, custodians, bus drivers, and others.
- Utilize a high school librarian for districtwide purchasing of library or media services.
- Employ out-of-district consultants to complete specific, one-time tasks at a cost less than maintaining a full-time staff person with those skills.
- Select teachers to coordinate curriculum development projects on a part-time basis.
- Utilize substitute teacher funds for such enrichment programs as films, guest speakers, and so forth. An absent teacher could elect either a substitute teacher for the class or enrichment program attendance.
- Expand the duties of teacher aides and paraprofessionals to the full extent allowed by law and regulations.
- Use paraprofessionals for study hall or corridor duty, allowing teachers more time for instruction.
- Change staffing patterns; replace an all-teacher physical education staff with a team made up of fewer teachers and more trained paraprofessionals for less pay.

P W I N O    2.26 Utilize volunteers for tutoring, grading papers, and other services.

P W I N O    2.27 Hire employees in cooperation with other agencies such as other school districts, education service districts, community colleges, city and county government, state department of human resources, and so on.

P W I N O    2.28 Reduce staff absenteeism (cutting health costs) by initiating or improving an employee wellness program. Contact your insurance agent of record for details.

## *Ideas That Reduce Expenditures without Necessarily Reducing Services*

P W I N O    2.29 Develop collective bargaining contracts carefully.
- Do not tie salary increases directly to the consumer price indexes; this may result in an escalation of salaries beyond the funds available.

- Sign a two- or three-year agreement with employees, but provide for a review of the economic package for the second and third years.
- Renegotiate salary schedules.
- Freeze or reduce all salaries for a specified period of time.
- Hold the same salary schedule for another year, but negotiate a total freeze including the step increase.
- Review and standardize salary and fringe benefit programs for all employees, eliminating costly exceptions.
- Coordinate fringe benefits (medical and major medical, dental, vision, and life insurance) in cases where both spouses work for the school district.
- Provide insurance coverage only for the employee.
- Negotiate for increases in fringe benefits in lieu of salary increases.
- Negotiate fringe benefit dollars, not benefits.
- Districts paying insurance premiums for teachers could initiate a wellness insurance plan, with a portion of premiums returned to each member who stays well.
- Freeze or reduce tuition reimbursement allowances.
- Freeze or reduce paid leaves.

P W I N O   2.30 Review personnel policies for possible savings. Consider such factors as staff development activities, professional growth requirements, and pay policies.

P W I N O   2.31 Implement a plan requiring that school district administrators develop specific written suggestions to reduce costs, and to improve efficiency and productivity.

P W I N O   2.32 Reduce the need for substitute teachers by minimizing teacher absenteeism. For example, one district removed its ceiling on accumulated sick leave, which significantly reduced absenteeism because employees knew that they would not "lose" sick leave hours.

P W I N O   2.33 Use temporary contracts for all new employees.

P W I N O   2.34 Hold off some teacher hiring until the start of the school year if elementary class sizes are not definite.

P W I N O      2.35 Hire personnel according to midyear enrollment projections (which tend to be lower) rather than projections for the beginning of the school year.

P W I N O      2.36 Conduct all in-service training during nonschool hours or on Saturdays.

P W I N O      2.37 Encourage all classes of employees to take early retirement by providing cash bonus or retroactive pay raise incentives. Provide early retirees with part-time employment opportunities. Increased staff turnover saves the dollar difference between top and entry-level salary schedules.

P W I N O      2.38 Adopt assertive termination procedures for those who cannot provide satisfactory services. In times of staff reduction, this could help retain excellent teachers who may be less experienced.

*Ideas That Reduce Expenditures by Reducing Services*

P W I N O      2.39 Determine whether the district is overstaffed and reduce staff where possible.
- Employ fewer specialists (music, physical education, special education, etc.).
- Reduce the number of sections offered at the secondary school level.
- Contract with a community college for advanced courses.
- Shift or combine assignments.

P W I N O      2.40 Freeze hiring or establish a strict review process for hiring new employees to replace those leaving.
- Do not replace personnel who have taken leaves of absence.

P W I N O      2.41 Reduce the number of administrators through multiassignments.
- Share an area specialist with other districts.
- Assign one principal to two schools, with a vice-principal or head teacher in each school.

- Assign principals to teach part time.
- Establish combined superintendent/principal positions.
- Combine curriculum supervision with evaluation supervision, and so on.

P W I N O    2.42 Decentralize district administration; eliminate district curriculum departments and replace them with assignments to school administrators and staff.

P W I N O    2.43 Reduce the need for substitute teachers by utilizing administrators and counselors in the classrooms (e.g., each administrator and counselor in the district might be required to serve in the classroom for three days during the year).

P W I N O    2.44 Assign one fewer substitute per day to each high school; e.g., eight teacher absences, seven substitutes.

P W I N O    2.45 Utilize classroom teacher/student advisors to supplement the high school counseling program.

P W I N O    2.46 Where possible, reduce full-time teaching and non-teaching positions to half time (e.g., librarian, home economics, foreign language, etc.).

P W I N O    2.47 Eliminate the number of specialist teachers with formal teaching loads and use them as resource teachers to assist regular classroom teachers.

## School-level Administration

P W I N O    2.48 Matters for consideration:
- Establish criteria for setting priorities.
- Consider ways to handle disruptive or handicapped students. Perhaps compulsory attendance rules need modification.
- Be prepared to respond to the claim that the "senior year" is a waste.
- Research ways to modify building schedules, keeping parent and student complaints to a minimum.
- Consider alternative energy sources and ways to economize.

- Find ways to deal with collective bargaining requirements.
- Find out if your state's Teachers Standards and Practices Commission will modify rules or grant waivers on assignments.

## Staff

P W I N O    2.49 Consider contract alternatives used by some districts.
- Reduce the number of days in contracts for administrators, teachers, and nonteaching staff (e.g., from 190 days to 187).
- Add vacation days without pay.
- Assign one certificated position to a program, assisted by volunteers and minimum-pay personnel.
- Cut back on the number of certificated supervisors.
- Utilize more part-time personnel.
- Utilize retired personnel more effectively.
- Contract with community college staff or part-time teachers to teach specialized courses at the junior or senior high school level where there is limited enrollment or a lack of staff expertise.
- Increase the use of student work programs.
- Assign fewer coaches per sport.
- Avoid duplication of classes offered at the middle and senior high schools.
- Analyze the need for temporary employees. Consider consolidating part-time functions into full-time positions; temporary employees can help with short-term needs.

P W I N O    2.50 Consider cost-saving measures that may involve a request for a waiver of the State Standards for Public Schools.
- Cut back on the number of days of instruction in the classroom by assigning students to outside research projects and individual study programs (field trips, etc.).
- Utilize a four-day workweek, with longer school days and additional work assignments.

- Delay purchasing textbooks if current programs are successful now; the state may be willing to grant independent adoptions or waivers.

P W I N O   2.51 Reduce extracurricular activities.

- Assign a minimum of one female, one male, and one coed activity in both the athletic and nonathletic areas for each quarter (fall, winter, spring).
- Reduce interschool activity schedules, including the number of activities, nonleague activities, and tournaments, and distances traveled.
- Encourage more home activities and organize fund-raisers to raise funds to offset the cost of the activity.

P W I N O   2.52 Reduce the number of electives. Consider scheduling a six-period day rather than seven periods or a block schedule.

P W I N O   2.53 Increase class size on a selective basis.

P W I N O   2.54 Offer driver training during the summer only on a self-supporting tuition basis.

## Building Schedules

P W I N O   2.55 Examine subject matter content and methods, and consider combining all three major high school science courses (biology, chemistry, physics) into a single integrated course that is scheduled over a three-year period, resulting in increased class size, fewer sections, and better use of science rooms and labs.

P W I N O   2.56 Combine several levels of the same content area into a single class; for example, second-, third-, and fourth-year foreign language classes could be taught during the same period.

P W I N O   2.57 Consider the twelve-month school year.

- Beneficial in a period of growth in student population.
- Added operating costs (custodial, administrative).
- Seems most acceptable to parents and students in lower grades.

P W I N O        2.58 Consider a daily class schedule that places all planning time at the beginning of each day; teachers then are available for assignment during class time.

## Transportation

P W I N O        2.59 Develop transportation patterns to reduce routes and frequency.

P W I N O        2.60 In districts with large numbers of students and a comparatively small geographical size, stagger class starting and dismissal times to better utilize drivers and buses.

P W I N O        2.61 Smaller districts with large distances to cover could eliminate early afternoon routes for the primary grades.

P W I N O        2.62 Increase the walking distance expected of students to school and bus stops.

P W I N O        2.63 Evaluate bus routes to be sure that buses are not duplicating one another, and that bus loading is distributed for greatest efficiency.

P W I N O        2.64 Reduce deadhead mileage by adding bus storage areas.

P W I N O        2.65 Stagger building schedules so that specialized staff can work in two or more buildings, and students can be transported more efficiently.

P W I N O        2.66 Reduce the frequency of early dismissals that require additional bus runs; dismiss all students at the same time to reduce runs.

P W I N O        2.67 Consider implementing "pod" or "clustered pickup points" for picking up or letting off students instead of offering door-to-door transportation.

## Staffing Patterns

P W I N O        2.68 Study staff assignments to minimize "misassignments," but when necessary, plan appropriate in-service programs to assist in shifting employees to new assignments.

P W I N O   2.69 Develop and use a current catalog of graduates, retired employees, and others in the community who may be willing to supplement instructional activities.

P W I N O   2.70 Develop, implement, and encourage a program designed to make use of community volunteers.

## Use of Buildings

P W I N O   2.71 Study buildings to make full use of all school facilities, including multipurpose and other instructional spaces.

P W I N O   2.72 Close wings or units of buildings by consolidating space.

P W I N O   2.73 Develop safety consciousness to reduce state accident insurance fund fees.

P W I N O   2.74 Consider setting up a fund for student activities that is used to pay for vandalism, with the balance available for student use.

P W I N O   2.75 Establish a realistic fee schedule for use of buildings by outside groups to at least recover the energy and custodial costs.

## Expanded Cost-saving Ideas

P W I N O   2.76 *Expanded Idea #1.* Negotiate the "real cost to district" for wages and related costs, rather than just for "increases in salary schedule."

P W I N O   2.77 *Expanded Idea #2.* Reward the entire staff for participating in a wellness program by offering an insurance rebate or by allowing staff to exercise during certain prescribed times.

P W I N O   2.78 *Expanded Idea #3.* Utilize current staff members as resource personnel for in-service training.

## CHAPTER 3: COST-SAVINGS TIPS FOR INSTRUCTIONAL SERVICES

### Curriculum Offerings

P W I N O  3.1 Conduct curriculum and course reviews to determine what can be eliminated, ranking programs by priority.

P W I N O  3.2 Examine subject matter and methods to determine the feasibility of combining multiple courses into a single class period—for example, second-, third-, and fourth-year foreign language together; pooled business education courses.

P W I N O  3.3 Offer classes on alternating years.

P W I N O  3.4 Charge fees for student participation in nonrequired classes.

### Organization

P W I N O  3.5 Eliminate kindergartens and provide structured activities for use in the home.

P W I N O  3.6 Several districts, jointly or with a community college, could operate the more expensive educational programs or an alternative school.

P W I N O  3.7 Approve early graduation for employed students and those ready for college-level work.

P W I N O  3.8 Provide other options for reluctant attendees; reentry with dignity into the school program should remain as a feasible option.

P W I N O  3.9 Allow more alternatives for credit: outside learning activities (private lessons or activities in music, athletics, art or drama; work experience), credit by examination, open entry/open exit courses, home-study programs (correspondence, computer, Internet, and television), and performance-based programs.

P W I N O  3.10 Allow students to take courses for credit by testing out of the course or demonstrating competency.

**Instruction**

*Use of Time*

P W I N O     3.11 Consider the optimum number of days needed to accomplish curriculum goals.

P W I N O     3.12 Consider year-round school.

P W I N O     3.13 Combine instruction in related subjects.

P W I N O     3.14 Establish a common staff preparation time prior to the arrival of students or after they leave.

P W I N O     3.15 Increase academic learning time to help raise student achievement levels.

P W I N O     3.16 Make the primary-age students' day longer to coordinate with the bus schedule, or consider a full day of instruction every other day.

*Staffing*

P W I N O     3.17 Analyze staff tasks to determine the most efficient ways to utilize employees and others (teachers, aides, volunteers, students, custodial, administrators, retired personnel, parents). Involve staff in suggesting ideas on cutting costs through such means as variable staffing patterns, flexible working hours, and use of funds for substitutes.

P W I N O     3.18 Volunteers might serve as monitors of halls, buses, and playgrounds in place of paid personnel, club and organization advisors, and aides. Reward service with golden age cards, free lunches, or some other type of special recognition.

P W I N O     3.19 Utilize parents and other volunteers to assist with in-school kindergarten or preschool activities.

P W I N O     3.20 Identify instructional programs in which students can receive instruction while performing a service for the school/district. For example, students in typing classes could produce school correspondence and bulletins.

P W I N O     3.21 Combine all levels of a particular sport for coaching and instruction.

P W I N O     3.22 Increase the teacher-pupil ratio for lecture classes.

P W I N O     3.23 Utilize cross-grade groupings.

P W I N O     3.24 Eighth-grade students could be moved into the high school to better utilize staff and space. (Perhaps the eighth-graders' schedule could be different from the high school schedule.)

*Space and Equipment*

P W I N O     3.25 Provide teachers with workspace, thus freeing classrooms for instructional purposes.

P W I N O     3.26 Lease out any unused facilities or equipment.

P W I N O     3.27 Where a facility or expertise is not available or would be unnecessarily duplicated, contract with the community (local offices, shops, hospitals, community college) to provide specialized instruction.

P W I N O     3.28 Consider leasing or the lease option to purchase of equipment, rather than outright purchase. Explore the possibility of equipment grants from businesses within the area.

P W I N O     3.29 Cooperatively purchase equipment used for short periods of time, rotating its use.

P W I N O     3.30 Review the use of telephones to determine their need. A central telephone may be adequate for most purposes.

*Scheduling*

P W I N O     3.31 Consider year-round school operation.

P W I N O     3.32 To conserve energy and expense, schedule school activities (e.g., athletics, music, and drama) during school hours, in the afternoon, or on Saturdays, instead of evenings.

*Materials*

P W I N O     3.33 Purchase only instructional materials that relate to specific instructional goals.

P W I N O    3.34 Provide incentives for teachers to become more cost-conscious in the use of instructional materials.

P W I N O    3.35 Establish a regional clearinghouse to coordinate distribution of used and surplus textbooks, and to fill shortages.

P W I N O    3.36 Consider using other relevant materials and the Internet to limit the number of textbooks needed.

P W I N O    3.37 Consider using self-instructional materials for individualized programs (computer-assisted instruction, instructional learning systems, videotape, learning packages).

P W I N O    3.38 Use outside resources to supplement school materials (local and state libraries, School Library Information Systems providing online access to electronic media in the form of newspapers, periodicals, etc., museums, businesses, and ESD materials centers).

## Vocational Education

*School Management*

P W I N O    3.39 Utilize any publications available from your department of education to review an existing, alternative, or new vocational program in terms of cost-effectiveness.

P W I N O    3.40 Use computers already in the school to help counselors with individual scheduling and program planning.

P W I N O    3.41 Utilize the online Career Information System (CIS) for individualized vocational counseling.

*Staffing*

P W I N O    3.42 Manufacturing technology (industrial arts) and vocational agriculture classes could be combined, eliminating the need for one teacher.

P W I N O    3.43 Reduce the duration of the vocational agriculture teacher's contract, from 240 days to 215, which still would allow for summer student project supervision and teacher in-service programs.

*Alternative Program Design*

P W I N O     3.44 Offer an open lab, with a teacher and an aide available to assist students—for example, individualized accounting and secretarial classes or welding.

P W I N O     3.45 Where the vocational needs of students cannot be met at school, contract with business interests to teach classes in offices, shops, and hospitals in the community. Develop cooperative programs with the local community college.

P W I N O     3.46 Avoid duplication of programs in adjacent school districts and in multiple high school districts; share programs, equipment and facilities.

P W I N O     3.47 Emphasize such programs as job shadowing, cooperative work experience, internships, and apprenticeships to minimize the need for facilities and expensive equipment.


*Self-supporting Programs*

P W I N O     3.48 Include a unit on food preparation and catering in the home economics, food service cluster, or restaurant/ tourism program catering for actual events in school and outside, which could pay for the food used in training.

P W I N O     3.49 Offer a manufacturing class, including the sale of student-manufactured goods. Investigate profit possibilities in entrepreneurial program activities.

P W I N O     3.50 Implement business incubators where students study how to start a small business, develop a business plan, and so forth for the first semester, and then choose one of the plans and put it into operation the second semester using the profits from the business to pay for the cost of the program and to leave seed money for the next year's class.

P W I N O     3.51 Utilize student initiative and leadership through student leadership organizations to earn money for needed equipment and supplies.

*Equipment and Supplies*

P W I N O    3.52 Utilize computers for word processing.

P W I N O    3.53 Solicit equipment contributions to school programs from local industry, state government, and so forth.

P W I N O    3.54 Acquire scrap materials from business and industry for classroom use, after which it can be returned to industry again to be sold as scrap.

P W I N O    3.55 Make children's and infants' clothing in home economics or clothing construction classes; fewer supplies are required.

P W I N O    3.56 Require that students pay a nonrefundable lost/broken tool fee.

*Advisory Committees*

P W I N O    3.57 Coordinate programs in such a way that an "umbrella-type" advisory committee could meet advisory committee requirements for high school, community college, and apprenticeship programs; ensure that membership is broad enough to accomplish the results desired.

**Special Education**

*Limitations on Services*

P W I N O    3.58 Use of stricter eligibility criteria would limit the number of handicapped students served. Those who are classified as marginally handicapped could be served through the regular school program.

P W I N O    3.59 Diagnostic evaluations could be limited to the minimum required by law.

P W I N O    3.60 Surveying the tests in use in district and schoolwide special education programs, and limiting tests used to a few standardized tests mutually agreed upon to save expenses.

*Staffing*

P W I N O    3.61 Special education teachers, serving as consultants to regular classroom teachers, could help develop and manage handicapped students' IEPs, and oversee the delivery of services using a "consultive model."

P W I N O    3.62 Hire teachers with special education certification as well as regular certification to teach in the regular class setting and provide special education services at the same time.

P W I N O    3.63 Expand the use of paraprofessionals; for example, instead of employing two teachers, employ one teacher and two aides.

P W I N O    3.64 Encourage high school and college students, parents, and other volunteers in the district to serve as aides or teaching assistants.

P W I N O    3.65 A special education teacher could handle more than one assignment; for example, a speech teacher also could serve as a speech/behavioral specialist.

P W I N O    3.66 When there are only a few students with a particular handicapping condition, these students could be served in other classes for handicapped students, using aides as necessary.

P W I N O    3.67 Join with other districts to deliver such services as physical therapy and occupational therapy.

P W I N O    3.68 Seek help from community groups; for example, service clubs can plan special projects to generate funds and provide other assistance.

*Current Practice*

When facing cutbacks in special education, it may be helpful to consider the following questions:

P W I N O    3.69 Does an existing situation require a change?

P W I N O    3.70 Are there only one to four students in one age group (elementary, junior high, high school) who need a special education program?

P W I N O    3.71 Have the funding sources decreased so that it is no longer feasible to have a few students in a categorical, self-contained class?

*Cost*

P W I N O    3.72 What is the current cost of operation?

P W I N O    3.73 What would the cost be with a new model?

P W I N O    3.74 What is the most economical way to group students?

*Personnel*

P W I N O    3.75 Can programs be eliminated rather than personnel even considering maintenance of effort regulations?

P W I N O    3.76 Can personnel be used in other ways—for example, as consultants rather than teachers?

P W I N O    3.77 Can current staff be used in a transdisciplinary approach?

P W I N O    3.78 Is in-service training available for new staff roles in new models of delivering special education services?

*Building Utilization*

P W I N O    3.79 Will as many school facilities be needed?

*Transportation*

P W I N O    3.80 Are students being transported in the most economical way possible?

P W I N O    3.81 Are students receiving services as close to home as possible? What are the placement options?

P W I N O    3.82 How do students move from one program to another in the district?

P W I N O    3.83 Will new eligibility data need to be gathered for new models?

P W I N O     3.84 Are models being developed that address the needs of the low-incidence students?

P W I N O     3.85 Can new models be developed without disturbing federal and state categorical funding channels?

## *Parents*

P W I N O     3.86 Will parents be involved in creating new models?

P W I N O     3.87 What will the extent of parent involvement be? What are the options?

P W I N O     3.88 Is a new model being developed that is functional?

P W I N O     3.89 Have the needs of the students and resources available been assessed, and how do these two factors compare or differ?

P W I N O     3.90 Have all options for models been explored?

P W I N O     3.91 Have any ideas been excluded?

P W I N O     3.92 Have the ideas allowed for openness and creativity?

## Guidance Programs

*Two Guiding Principles*

Those who already have had to grapple with the dilemma of shrinking resources have found that:

P W I N O     3.93 Program quality is preserved best by utilizing the most effective techniques available for delivery of instruction and services.

P W I N O     3.94 Curtailing each program somewhat may be better than eliminating one or more programs altogether.

*Limit Programs without Permanently Crippling Services to Students*

P W I N O     3.95 Assign counselors, administrators, and other support personnel as "duty substitutes" for one day per week.

P W I N O     3.96 Assign one period of teaching per day to six non-teaching staff members, saving the cost of one FTE teaching position.

P W I N O     3.97 Using the "critical time" principle, save the funds spent on extended contracts for counselors, administrators, librarians, and other nonteaching staff members.

P W I N O     3.98 Careful analysis of the work performed by an individual may show that someone else could assume some of the duties.

P W I N O     3.99 Save one-third FTE by utilizing an intern counselor, teacher, administrator, or similar personnel when a vacancy occurs.

P W I N O     3.100 While it is not cost effective over the long run, the district could temporarily discontinue paying for staff travel, in-service training, attendance at conferences, supplementary materials, and college tuition.

P W I N O     3.101 Save FTE by having counselors teach guidance-related classes, such as career education, career awareness, etc.

**Media Services**

*Administration*

P W I N O     3.102 Give the district media coordinator more responsibility to coordinate and implement cost-saving ideas within the district media program to eliminate unnecessary duplication and procedures.

P W I N O     3.103 Consider the advantages and disadvantages of centralizing selected activities at the district level: purchase of materials, textbooks and workbooks, printing services, the production of materials, cataloging.

P W I N O     3.104 Consider the pros and cons of unifying the school and public library.

P W I N O     3.105 When implementing federal and state program requirements to establish resource centers for Title I, and similar programs, consider integration with existing media center facilities and management systems.

P W I N O     3.106 Schools should contact ESDs and other agencies for coordinating cost-saving services and information.

P W I N O     3.107 Consider a central depository for rarely used materials. Such cooperation may be feasible within a district, between several districts, or through an ESD.

P W I N O     3.108 Be sure a materials selection policy is developed and implemented for the district.

P W I N O     3.109 Eliminate cataloging at the building level.

P W I N O     3.110 Consider installing an electronic security system in the media center.

P W I N O     3.111 Consider the pros and cons of computerizing and automating the card catalog.

P W I N O     3.112 Keep current on developments in instructional technology for media programs and instruction (e.g., computers in schools, etc.)

P W I N O     3.113 Conduct a flea market and sell items (books, authorized equipment, small furniture, etc.) that are no longer needed or used by the school.

P W I N O     3.114 Consider the pros and cons of collecting fees on lost, damaged, or stolen books, or require students to perform work to repay costs incurred.

P W I N O     3.115 Seek out donations for materials and funds from public and private sources.

## Services

P W I N O     3.116 When applicable, obtain copyright release to reprint only those portions of textbooks and supplementary materials that are used in the district's instructional program.

P W I N O     3.117 Consider the cost-effectiveness of photocopying as opposed to offset printing.

P W I N O     3.118 If you have not already done so, consider the use of videocassettes in place of 16mm format.

P W I N O    3.119 Encourage teachers to utilize in-school television programming, provided at no charge by several national programs.

P W I N O    3.120 Consider the applications of computers in the media centers for library management applications, as well as for instructional and research purposes.

*Materials*

P W I N O    3.121 Arrange for increased resource sharing among schools, districts, ESDs, and such other agencies as public libraries, community colleges, or special libraries.

P W I N O    3.122 Consider cooperative purchasing of materials, periodicals: within districts, between districts, through ESDs, or through regional organizations.

P W I N O    3.123 Evaluate frequency of use of periodicals; prioritize them according to use and need; discontinue low priority subscriptions.

P W I N O    3.124 When older books (library materials and textbooks) will continue to be used, consider rebinding rather than purchasing new copies.

P W I N O    3.125 Consider a temporary moratorium on the purchase of books for a given curriculum area. Subscriptions for periodicals and newspapers should be maintained.

P W I N O    3.126 Weed materials collections of old, outdated materials.

*Equipment*

P W I N O    3.127 Purchase expensive equipment cooperatively.

P W I N O    3.128 Investigate the pros and cons of equipment maintenance contracts.

P W I N O    3.129 Consider the advantages and disadvantages of a lease option when purchasing equipment.

P W I N O    3.130 When cost effective, use shop classes or projects to build items for the media center/school.

P W I N O    3.131 Consolidate media equipment repair for several districts.

P W I N O    3.132 Refinish furniture or equipment rather than making new purchases.

P W I N O    3.133 When cost effective, store equipment and materials from schools that are temporarily closed.

## Cost-saving Ideas

*Curriculum*

P W I N O    3.134 *Expanded Idea #1.* High schools offer specialized science courses to relatively small numbers of students, making science instruction an area of high cost. A well-coordinated science program can be developed that will reduce costs while providing a complete high school science curriculum.

*Instruction*

P W I N O    3.135 *Expanded Idea #2.* Many of the tasks currently assigned to administrators, when broken down into small jobs, can be carried out by paraprofessionals following short-term training. This requires precise analysis of job descriptions, so that responsibilities can be itemized.

P W I N O    3.136 *Expanded Idea #3.* It has been found that if the amount of time spent directly on learning a task can be increased, there is a significant chance that student achievement levels can be increased. The best method of increasing learning time is to improve classroom management and provide direct instruction.

P W I N O    3.137 *Expanded Idea #4.* A clearinghouse system can be established for textbooks that are available, in surplus, or for which there is a shortage.

*Vocational Education*

P W I N O     3.138 *Expanded Idea #5.* Limit the specialized vocational education program to the junior/senior level, and teach only those occupational skills that are considered vital for entering the labor market using studies such as the SCANS report to identify vital occupational skills.

P W I N O     3.139 *Expanded Idea #6.* Two or more school districts could offer a joint program, available to all students.

*Special Education*

P W I N O     3.140 *Expanded Idea #7.* Combine two classes, each with a teacher and an aide, into one class with one teacher and two aides.

P W I N O     3.141 *Expanded Idea #8.* Combine severely and moderately handicapped students in a classroom with one teacher and one aide.

P W I N O     3.142 *Expanded Idea #9.* Districts may be able to cut costs by contracting for specific instructional services that, in the past, have been provided by on-staff personnel.

*Student Services*

P W I N O     3.143 *Expanded Idea #10.* Utilize support personnel as substitute teachers. Assign counselors, administrators, and other support personnel for "duty substitute" one day per week; for example, if a substitute is needed Monday, one counselor serves while other counselors remain on assignment; if a substitute is needed Tuesday, another counselor serves, and so on.

P W I N O     3.144 *Expanded Idea #11.* Have guidance staff teach related courses. In the last fifteen years, a number of districts in Oregon, for example, have maintained a moderately staffed guidance program by utilizing counselors to teach courses.

P W I N O  3.145 *Expanded Idea #12.* Utilize a paraprofessional to perform many duties that do not require professional expertise.

P W I N O  3.146 *Expanded Idea #13.* Utilize teachers to provide guidance services (e.g., "Guide Program—assign guidance responsibilities to be shared among teaching staff.).

P W I N O  3.147 *Expanded Idea #14.* Use a "Mobile Guidance Unit" to provide guidance and counseling services to small rural school districts or schools within a district.

P W I N O  3.148 *Expanded Idea #15.* Analyze procedures for assisting some students to make a successful transition to alternative education programs. Assist these students to seek education or work through private programs supported by flow-through from basic school support funds or jobs in business and industry.

P W I N O  3.149 *Expanded Idea #16.* Have counselors work with the emotionally handicapped. Utilize one or more counselors to work part-time with emotionally handicapped students in a class room. These students could carry as much of the regular program as possible, while attending this class one or two periods daily.

## Media Services

P W I N O  3.150 *Expanded Idea #17.* The district media coordinator could be given the authority to handle the ordering and use of expensive items on a districtwide basis; in some cases, this may involve close coordination with building administrators.

P W I N O  3.151 *Expanded Idea #18.* For periodicals, it may be possible to obtain additional discounts from subscription service agencies through cooperative purchasing arrangements or to purchase subscription services on line such as EBESCO. Such arrangements may be within districts, between districts, through ESDs, or through regional organizations.

P W I N O  3.152 *Expanded Idea #19.* Consider rebinding old and damaged textbooks, as well as other instructional materials, rather than replacing them with new copies.

P W I N O       3.153 *Expanded Idea #20.* Install electronic security systems in media centers.

P W I N O       3.154 *Expanded Idea #21.* Consider unifying the school and public libraries.

P W I N O       3.155 *Expanded Idea #22.* Out-of-date or seldom-used materials should be removed selectively from the media center and classrooms. Such removal allows for additional shelf space and more efficient use of the media center.

P W I N O       3.156 *Expanded Idea #23.* The district should develop a districtwide materials selection policy to assure that only relevant materials are purchased to support the curriculum and leisure reading needs of students and teachers.

P W I N O       3.157 *Expanded Idea #24.* Teachers should be encouraged to utilize in-school television curriculum provided by the various satellite networks, Cable in the Classroom, V-Tel, and in many states, the department of education either has its own network, or broadcasts via the state's Public Broadcasting Service.


## CHAPTER 4: COST-SAVING TIPS FOR SUPPORT SERVICES

### Buildings and Grounds

*Energy Conservation*

P W I N O       4.1 In this era of high fuel prices, a comprehensive energy conservation program for the district is an absolute necessity.

P W I N O       4.2 Periodically reemphasize ongoing energy conservation programs.

P W I N O       4.3 Ask the local power company to conduct an on-site energy audit of the school building.

P W I N O       4.4 Ask the mechanical engineer who originally designed equipment for the building to evaluate the effectiveness of heating controls. Large districts might train their maintenance staff to repair the controls for heating and ventilating systems.

P W I N O    4.5 Save heating costs significantly by starting the school earlier in the year (e.g., in the middle of August), and extending Christmas vacation for two weeks before Christmas. Secondary students could seek temporary employment and school maintenance could be accomplished during that time.

P W I N O    4.6 Install heating and ventilating systems controlled by computer; such systems can help make better use of energy.

P W I N O    4.7 Improve heat energy sources through energy grants. Consider a change from diesel heating fuel to wood pellet, and so forth or consider the use of geothermal sources, if available, to heat your school.

P W I N O    4.8 Now that solar technology has improved, installations are proving more cost effective than originally predicted. For example, swimming pool and shower water can be solar heated in Oregon from May through mid-October. In this regard, solar system suppliers are becoming more competitive and districts should research all possibilities.

P W I N O    4.9 Consolidate the use of space, such as closing wings or units of buildings to save on heating and ventilating costs.

P W I N O    4.10 Continue replacement of incandescent lighting with fluorescent in schools. Although short-term capital expenditures are necessary, fluorescent lighting will reduce costs in the long run.

P W I N O    4.11 Disconnect electrical appliances (e.g., refrigerators, freezers) during summer vacation.

## Use of Buildings

P W I N O    4.12 Schedule building space and let groups know when space is available for community use. Have someone on duty one or two nights a week.

P W I N O    4.13 Consider using the high school as a community center, since it is one of the most frequently used buildings in the community. Include a number of activities normally scheduled at the local elementary school.

P W I N O     4.14 Adult education courses provided in school facilities could be charged the full fee, including utility expenditures.

P W I N O     4.15 Explore whether the use of facilities by special interest groups is appropriate.

P W I N O     4.16 Explore the joint use of facilities with other governmental agencies. Allow them to use spaces that are unoccupied at the present time, separating them from areas used by staff and students, and providing separate entrances to the building. Amortize the capital outlay required for remodeling over a five-year period. Share costs of building operations with other occupants.

## *Maintenance of Buildings*

P W I N O     4.17 Districts traditionally have emphasized the need for continuing professional growth of certificated staff through seminars, workshops, and additional academic credit. However, regular training for classified employees often is overlooked. Continuous employee training and periodic performance reviews are two important techniques for cost savings with custodial and light maintenance personnel.

P W I N O     4.18 Roof maintenance is a very technical matter and funds often are wasted on roofing programs that are not well conceived. Established criteria are needed for the selection of a roofer, particularly when working with built-up roofs. In cases where a roofer has done work for the district previously, determine the quality of that work and always seek references with whom you can discuss the quality of roofers' previous work.

P W I N O     4.19 Evaluate maintenance costs to determine whether repairs should be done by the staff or on contract; consider the cost effectiveness of replacement instead of repairs.

P W I N O     4.20 Contract maintenance and custodial programs.

P W I N O     4.21 Purchase products that are designed to reduce vandalism.

*Cleaning of Buildings*

P W I N O    4.22 A good relationship between custodial and other staff members can effectively cut costs. When classrooms are kept orderly, much less work is required of the custodian. Removal of chalk dust is appreciated by the teaching staff. The teachers should report to the custodian routine maintenance tasks that are needed, and the principal periodically should inspect the buildings with the custodian to see that standards are maintained.

P W I N O    4.23 A list of technical experts should be available so that district staff can obtain specialized help when it is needed.

P W I N O    4.24 Factors to consider when contracting for custodial services include cost, the size of the facility, facility construction and the types of programs conducted in that facility. Thoroughly analyze the job responsibilities of current staff to determine where contracted services are warranted; carefully determine whether contracting would impede the flexibility of facility use or staff and student interrelationships with those providing custodial services. Security is yet another consideration.

P W I N O    4.25 Use staff development programs to prepare custodial employees to assume added responsibilities.

P W I N O    4.26 Any changes in the maintenance program or operating schedules need to be agreed upon by the building principal, the custodian, and the central office personnel responsible for the maintenance of all facilities.

P W I N O    4.27 Look at major work schedules to determine how much time should be spent on certain tasks. Establishing uniform time periods required to perform particular tasks should be encouraged.

P W I N O    4.28 Custodians could work split shifts; that is, they could come to school and open the building, do some preliminary work, go home, and then return to school at the end of the day to do some sweeping.

P W I N O    4.29 Clean shops once a week, including home economics rooms. The vocational program areas could be cleaned as part of student training, leaving only maintenance activities to the custodial staff.

P W I N O    4.30 Science teachers should ask students to clean up the laboratory as part of the program. Equipment should be stored when not in use; custodians should not be expected to work with the equipment due to the possibility of damage.

P W I N O    4.31 Some of the new floor waxes act as a one-step cleaner and waxer, saving significantly on the cost of stripping floors.

P W I N O    4.32 Explore the utilization of unemployed individuals to assist with cleaning.

## Grounds Use and Maintenance

P W I N O    4.33 Investigate the feasibility of contracting for grounds maintenance.

P W I N O    4.34 Explore the utilization of community volunteers to maintain flowerbeds and shrubs on the school grounds.

P W I N O    4.35 Select low-maintenance plantings that are not placed in the way of the lawn mower.

P W I N O    4.36 Implement an ongoing, efficient program of weed control to avoid problems in this area.

P W I N O    4.37 Maintain blacktop in good condition; once it is allowed to deteriorate, repairs are costly. A system is needed for regular repair of chuckholes or fractures in the blacktop when they appear.

P W I N O    4.38 Consider the possibility of allowing large grass fields to go brown during summer months.

P W I N O    4.39 Install low-maintenance, yet safe, playground apparatus.

## Equipment Use and Maintenance

P W I N O    4.40 When equipment is purchased, find out the availability and cost of repairs.

P W I N O 4.41 Develop five-year maintenance schedules, updated each year, noting the activities that need to be carried out during that time and the cost.

P W I N O 4.42 Keep records on maintenance of repair, using a card file on large items of equipment (costing more than $500).

P W I N O 4.43 Train maintenance staff to repair furniture and equipment. Teach furniture refinishing as part of the wood shop course, letting students do the work.

P W I N O 4.44 A process is needed for reporting possible safety concerns to maintenance staff.

P W I N O 4.45 Analyze telephone service, evaluating the need for each extension. Reduce extensions where possible.

## Pupil Transportation

*Routes and Schedules*

P W I N O 4.46 Bus routes should be evaluated periodically to ensure that they are not overlapping one another, and that loads are distributed for greatest efficiency.

P W I N O 4.47 Larger buses and longer routes may be a consideration.

P W I N O 4.48 Deadhead mileage can be reduced by adding bus storage areas.

P W I N O 4.49 Staggering schedules allows for better utilization of buses and drivers.

P W I N O 4.50 In a district with a large enrollment in a relatively compact geographic area, staggering class schedules allows for better use of buses and driver time.

P W I N O 4.51 A small district covering a large geographic area could eliminate early afternoon routes for primary grade students.

P W I N O 4.52 Scheduling all students for one regular dismissal time can eliminate the need for duplicate runs.

P W I N O 4.53 Schedule kindergarten students to travel home with older students or eliminate noon runs and ask parents to be responsible for picking up students. Daylong kindergarten on alternating days could be considered, as well as a four-day school week for primary students.

P W I N O   4.54 Increasing students' walking distance to school and bus stops, while felt by many to be the best way to cut costs, may prove highly controversial.

## *Activity Trips*

P W I N O   4.55 The number of trips can be reduced; trips and events can be coordinated so that buses carry full loads.

P W I N O   4.56 Establishing the minimum and maximum distances allowed for field trips and making each educational unit or program responsible for trip expenses can yield savings.

P W I N O   4.57 Use a Telexplorer, an amplified telephone, developed for conference calls, as a viable alternative to field trips, or use two-way interactive video/television or the Internet to conduct a virtual field trip instead of actually traveling to the site.

P W I N O   4.58 Consider cutting all field trips.

## *School Bus Operation*

P W I N O   4.59 Some states still have union high school districts. Small component districts in a union high district can consolidate fleets; for example, some districts operate on a cooperative basis, others contract with the union high district for services, while still others utilize a single bus contractor in common.

P W I N O   4.60 Convert from gasoline to propane, or gasoline to diesel.

P W I N O   4.61 Investigate the feasibility of contracting for bus service.

P W I N O   4.62 Insurance programs should be reviewed and all options investigated for reduced costs for coverage. Consider bidding bus fleet insurance.

*Driver Training*

P W I N O     4.63 Driving for fuel economy can produce surprising cost savings.

P W I N O     4.64 Promote good driving habits: shorter warm-up periods, smooth starts and stops, driving at steady speeds, and so forth.

P W I N O     4.65 Use deadhead route mileage and time for driver training; experienced drivers can assist with behind-the-wheel training for new drivers.

P W I N O     4.66 Consider eliminating driver education altogether, subcontracting these services, or teaching behind–the-wheel programs in the summer time only.

*Equipment and Maintenance*

P W I N O     4.67 Purchase equipment that provides for the least expense over its entire life.

P W I N O     4.68 Even though an initial investment for radial tires is more than for other types of tires, some districts have found them cost effective in terms of increased mileage and reduced fuel and maintenance costs.

P W I N O     4.69 Electronic ignition systems can reduce maintenance costs by lengthening ignition component life.

**Food Services**

P W I N O     4.70 Programs can operate on a totally self-supporting basis.

P W I N O     4.71 They can operate within an established budget.

P W I N O     4.72 The district can establish a per meal cost and underwrite all costs above that figure.

P W I N O     4.73 The district can underwrite all costs as a part of the total expense of educating students and serve meals at no charge to students.

P W I N O    4.74 The district may choose to not offer a program.

P W I N O    4.75 Plan menus to make full use of commodities. Do a menu item cost analysis and reduce the frequency that high cost items appear on the menu. Cost account the entire menu to establish a balance between production costs and income. Utilize cycle menus, preferably seventeen-day cycles.

P W I N O    4.76 Purchase food from a planned menu cycle. Purchase in quantity, as much as storage will allow economically. Avoid "settling in" with one supplier for convenience, as this can be costly. Shop for good prices; food suppliers are in a competitive business and schools represent very desirable accounts.

P W I N O    4.77 For a cost-effective program, three types of storage areas are needed: frozen, cold, dry. Keep inventories in each area current as food is received and used. Store items most often used toward the entrance, least used in the rear. A security system will help avoid losses. Temperature controls for the frozen and cold storage areas should be safeproofed. Mice, insects, and dampness contaminate food, and precautions are relatively inexpensive when compared to the costs of food lost.

P W I N O    4.78 A good cost accounting system is essential; otherwise, large and unexpected deficits may occur. Cost accounting must be done at the building level, through the food service director and business manager.

P W I N O    4.79 Review the film training program "Efficient School Food Production."

P W I N O    4.80 Production records are the best safeguard from the over- and underproduction of food. Overproduction drives up per meal costs; underproduction reduces income and discourages participation. Production records are essential for accurate planning.

P W I N O    4.81 Make full use of USDA donated commodities, regular and bonus.

P W I N O      4.82 A lunch period that is truly a lunch period is advisable. Scheduling numerous activities at that time decreases participation in the lunch program. Staggering of lunch periods has helped increase student participation in the school nutrition program of many schools.

P W I N O      4.83 When pricing meals, students should be charged the actual cost of per meal preparation less the total of (a) state matching per meal revenue plus (b) federal per meal reimbursement plus (c) federal commodity per meal value. All adults should be charged at least the actual cost of per meal preparation.

P W I N O      4.84 School districts should avoid having income siphoned from school food services to others during the lunch period, such as student stores, vending machines, food sales, and so forth.

P W I N O      4.85 School nutrition program income comes from basically five sources: monies from paying students and adults, federal reimbursement, federally donated commodities, state matching monies, and local school district subsidy. Increased average daily participation increases income in the first four categories.

## Expanded Cost-saving Ideas

*Buildings and Grounds*

P W I N O      4.86 *Expanded Idea #1.* Often, several buildings in a school district are open on the same night, with only a minimum of student or community activities scheduled for each. Scheduling activities in the fewest number of buildings practicable saves custodial and energy costs.

P W I N O      4.87 *Expanded Idea #2.* Lease or rent surplus building space. Extra income can be earned by school districts if they rent or lease the vacant space in these school buildings.

P W I N O      4.88 *Expanded Idea #3.* Equipment and facilities owned by school districts should be maintained according to a five-year schedule.

*Transportation*

P W I N O    4.89 *Expanded Idea #4*. Purchase diesel-powered buses whenever replacement or additional vehicles are needed.

P W I N O    4.90 *Expanded Idea #5*. Convert some of buses from gasoline fuel to propane; most properly converted vehicles yield cost savings.

P W I N O    4.91 *Expanded Idea #6*. Additional starting and dismissal times allow for increased utilization of existing buses, resulting in significant savings.

P W I N O    4.92 *Expanded Idea #7*. Consolidation of fleets is an approach used by several districts to reduce transportation costs; this is particularly effective in union high school districts or in relatively small geographic areas where there are two or more adjoining districts.

P W I N O    4.93 *Expanded Idea #8*. Since only certain types of pupil transportation are required, it is possible to eliminate most of the school bus programs in the majority of districts; at least two districts have done this in recent years.

## Energy Conservation in School Transportation

P W I N O    4.94 Coordinate school calendars and start and dismissal times between schools of each school system.

P W I N O    4.95 Eliminate staggered dismissal times in the same building.

P W I N O    4.96 Increase requirements for walking distances to school and to bus stops.

P W I N O    4.97 Establish take-up and dismissal schedules at schools to support maximum vehicle utilization.

P W I N O    4.98 Eliminate buses for detention students.

P W I N O    4.99 Limit student parking, encourage high school pupils to ride school buses, form car pools, and so on.

P W I N O    4.100 For districts or schools that are close together geographically, establish maximum distances for cocurricular trips (say 60 miles round trip).

P W I N O  4.101 Utilize public mass transit where feasible to avoid duplication of service.

P W I N O  4.102 Establish travel restrictions for school sponsored activities supporting athletic teams. (Cheerleaders, band, pep clubs, rooters, etc.)

P W I N O  4.103 Eliminate buses for athletic team practices.

## School Bus Operation: Activity and Field Trips

P W I N O  4.104 Reduce or eliminate all but the most necessary athletic contests.

P W I N O  4.105 Reduce or eliminate all but the most necessary cocurricular trips.

P W I N O  4.106 Combine cocurricular and athletic trips for more than one school.

P W I N O  4.107 Have districts share buses when feasible.

P W I N O  4.108 Establish minimum and maximum distances for all trips.

P W I N O  4.109 Limit cocurricular trips to full busloads only.

P W I N O  4.110 Combine athletic schedules so several games can be played at the same time.

P W I N O  4.111 Encourage parents to carpool with other parents in transporting children to school for late activities and for extracurricular activities.

P W I N O  4.112 Contract with parents to provide transportation when feasible, but check on the liabilities involved with your legal counsel and insurance carrier or agent of record..

P W I N O  4.113 Utilize public transportation on return trips where feasible rather than return school buses to schools or homes.

## School Bus Operation: General

P W I N O  4.114 Lengthen distances between pick-up points.

P W I N O     4.115 Establish collection points.

P W I N O     4.116 Plan stops on level areas instead of on inclines.

P W I N O     4.117 Consolidate loads.

P W I N O     4.118 Plan routes to make only right-hand turns, to save on idling time, where safety permits.

P W I N O     4.119 Use intercoms and cameras on buses to reduce stops for controlling discipline.

P W I N O     4.120 Install trip recorders to record and monitor driver and vehicle operation when necessary.

P W I N O     4.121 Use smallest available vehicle for long-distance, light-load runs.

P W I N O     4.122 Install two-way radios to direct operation or redirection of buses to avoid unnecessary use.

P W I N O     4.123 Route buses to stay on main roads as much as possible.


*School Bus Routing and Scheduling*

P W I N O     4.124 Fill buses to legal capacity.

P W I N O     4.125 When replacing buses or expanding fleet, purchase buses with capacities to provide balanced fleet utilization.

P W I N O     4.126 Utilize proven updating routing techniques, either by hand or computer to maintain maximum vehicle utilization at all times.
a. Evaluate current system.
b. Revise system to reduce mileage, stops, and student riding time and distance.
c. Review policy and revise where needed.

P W I N O     4.127 Consolidate interdistrict transportation systems when possible to meet special transportation demands.

P W I N O     4.128 Develop an alternate routing plan for implementation in emergencies and fuel shortages.

*School Bus Operation: The Driver*

P W I N O    4.129 Retain experienced drivers as long as possible.

P W I N O    4.130 Reeducate bus drivers toward better fuel economy.

P W I N O    4.131 Reduce warm-up time on buses to two minutes initially, and three minutes prior to starting routes.

P W I N O    4.132 Drive slowly the first few miles until vehicle warms up.

P W I N O    4.133 Avoid full-throttle operation. Drive at steady speeds.

P W I N O    4.134 Avoid the "red line" even in shifting gears.

P W I N O    4.135 Drive slowly back to the bus garage. Turn corners slowly.

P W I N O    4.136 Reduce speed limit to as low as practical.

P W I N O    4.137 Avoid courtesy (unauthorized) stops.

P W I N O    4.138 Train new drivers on existing runs while bus is "deadheading."

P W I N O    4.139 Use simulators to reduce behind-the-wheel training in vehicles.

P W I N O    4.140 Increase frequency of driver in-service programs.

P W I N O    4.141 Hold joint workshops with drivers and mechanics to improve transportation operation.

P W I N O    4.142 Use an incentive system for reducing vehicle fuel consumption.

P W I N O    4.143 Review driver times and routes. Determine most efficient vehicle utilization, layover and storage plan to minimize miles for school as well as personal vehicles.

P W I N O    4.144 Keep foot off accelerator when the bus is stopped and off brakes when in motion. Reduce braking by anticipating stops.

*School Bus Maintenance*

P W I N O    4.145 Tune and maintain engines, plugs, points, and timing.

P W I N O    4.146 Maintain and clean pollution controls.

P W I N O    4.147 Keep gas tanks full to avoid excessive evaporation.

P W I N O    4.148 Avoid fuel spillage when refueling buses. Do not overfill.

P W I N O    4.149 Replace buses that use excessive amounts of fuel as soon as economically feasible.

P W I N O    4.150 Keep gasoline tanks locked with one person in charge of fueling of buses and other school vehicles.

P W I N O    4.151 Keep accurate bus records for maintenance and fuel consumption.

P W I N O    4.152 Analyze record data for potential management decisions to achieve savings.

P W I N O    4.153 Inventory all parts and supplies and order for a full year on a planned-need basis, with best price on past experiences.

P W I N O    4.154 In winter, keep all buses under cover rather than allowing drivers to take them home and park.

P W I N O    4.155 Use engine warmers for easier starts.

P W I N O    4.156 Maintain clean oil and air filters.

P W I N O    4.157 Keep automatic choke clean. A sticking choke will waste fuel.

P W I N O    4.158 Keep air-fuel mixture or carburetor precisely adjusted.

P W I N O    4.159 Regulate oil change with engine tune-up.

P W I N O    4.160 Use manufacturer's recommended weight of oil.

P W I N O    4.161 Check tire balance and wheel alignment to avoid "drag," which will use more fuel and shorten tire life.

P W I N O    4.162 Check radiator thermostat. A defective thermostat may prolong engine warm up, increasing fuel consumption.

P W I N O    4.163 Use proper octane rated fuel. Using wrong octane will result in plug foul up and reduction of mileage; using higher octane is a waste of money.

P W I N O    4.164 Use engine analyzing equipment to assure maximum efficiency.

P W I N O    4.165 Make full utilization of service manuals and maintenance bulletins to keep updated on maintenance techniques.

P W I N O    4.166 Take full advantage of free maintenance training clinics conducted by skilled instructors.

P W I N O    4.167 Keep brakes properly adjusted.

P W I N O    4.168 Repair engine oil leaks.

P W I N O    4.169 Install radiator shutters for retaining engine heat.

P W I N O    4.170 Install radial tires.

P W I N O    4.171 Retrofit ignition with electronic ignition system.

P W I N O    4.172 Properly utilize proven fuel and oil additives.

P W I N O    4.173 Maintain proper tire pressure.

P W I N O    4.174 Utilize new techniques such as rubber suspension systems, wheel balancers, tire pressure equalizers, solid state ignition, and so forth.

## Transportation Office and Garage

P W I N O    4.175 Maintain lighting fixtures (a clean fixture in good working order can deliver up to 50 percent more light).

P W I N O    4.176 Clean walls and ceilings and/or paint with light flat or semigloss finish.

P W I N O    4.177 Turn off all lights and other electrical equipment when not in use.

P W I N O    4.178 Reduce exterior lighting to lowest level consistent with good security and safety.

P W I N O    4.179 Perform janitorial services earlier so that electricity may be turned off earlier.

P W I N O    4.180 Check all equipment and motors. Adjust belts for proper tension; turn off when not in use.

P W I N O    4.181 Limit the use of electrical space heaters.

P W I N O    4.182 Tighten and clean all electrical connections from the circuit breakers back through the transformers to the main switch.

P W I N O    4.183 Consider the installation of photocell controllers to turn exterior lights on and off.

P W I N O     4.184 Concentrate evening work/meetings in a single heating/cooling zone instead of heating or cooling the whole office or garage.

P W I N O     4.185 Clean up heat exchanger and heating oil surfaces for better heat transfer, change filters at regular intervals, clean fan blades and damper blades.

P W I N O     4.186 Request visitors and staff to avoid introduction of adverse conditions by opening windows or holding open doors.

P W I N O     4.187 Consider the installation of added insulation to building walls and ceiling to decrease heat transfer.

P W I N O     4.188 Consider the installation of insulated glass in place of single-pane glass.

P W I N O     4.189 Consider the installation of weather-stripping, caulking, automatic door closers, and so on to decrease infiltration of outside air.

P W I N O     4.190 Close off all unnecessary openings — unused exhaust fans, broken windows, structural openings.

P W I N O     4.191 Replace grossly oversized motors.

P W I N O     4.192 Utilize blower system to circulate warm air from the ceiling to the floor of work areas.

P W I N O     4.193 Remove thermostats located near doors, windows, or heat producing sources.

P W I N O     4.194 Reduce thermostat setting on weekends, holidays, and at night.

P W I N O     4.195 Explore the use of Telexplorer, V-Tel, or conference calls in lieu of field trips or meetings.

## CHAPTER 5: COST SAVINGS FOR COMMUNITY COLLEGES

### Increased Revenue, Productivity, or Efficiency

*New Sources of Revenue*

P W I N O     5.1 Charge laboratory fees for computer programming and other courses usually not considered lab courses.

P W I N O  5.2 Establish fees for catalogs, transcripts, job search workshops, and parking.

P W I N O  5.3 Pursue private tax deductible donations to a foundation you set up for such purposes as endowed chairs, new facilities, and scholarships.

P W I N O  5.4 Open an electronic games center on campus, committing profits to intercollegiate athletics.

P W I N O  5.5 Eliminate third-party food service arrangements, opting to run the service with district employees or to use vending machines exclusively.

P W I N O  5.6 Revoke senior citizens' tuition waiver policy.

### Productivity and Efficiency Efforts

P W I N O  5.7 Combine small departments; eliminate some department head positions; place greater responsibility on associate deans for direct supervision.

P W I N O  5.8 Share employees with other agencies, such as school districts and city and county governments.

P W I N O  5.9 Disconnect and reduce the number of telephone lines on campus.

P W I N O  5.10 Consider a private telephone system, independent of larger carriers.

P W I N O  5.11 Contract for bookstore operations, custodial services, groundskeeping, and other services if cost savings can be effected.

P W I N O  5.12 Utilize volunteers for tutoring, grading papers, and other services.

P W I N O  5.13 Improve accident prevention efforts to reduce state accident insurance fund (SAIF) premiums.

P W I N O  5.14 Utilize criminal justice students as security guards for the campus.

P W I N O  5.15 Review and analyze forms used on campus, eliminating some, consolidating others.

P W I N O     5.16 Encourage energy conservation:
- Initiate an intensive weatherization program for doors and windows.
- Reevaluate lighting in all buildings: remove some night lights and reduce lighting where light of reading intensity is not needed.
- Investigate the feasibility of installing a computer-assisted energy management system.
- Place solar panels on building roofs to supplement space heating and hot water production.
- Monitor temperature in facilities, seeking energy savings where possible.
- Change outside campus parking lights to high-presence sodium.
- "Last one out, please turn out the lights!" signs above all light switches.

## Deferred and/or Reduced Expenditures

P W I N O     5.17 Place a freeze on all out-of-state travel and reduce out-of-district travel dramatically.

P W I N O     5.18 Avoid hiring a replacement for personnel on sabbatical leave.

P W I N O     5.19 Close the campus on Friday and Saturday during summer term.

P W I N O     5.20 Place a freeze or strict review process on hiring employees to replace those leaving the institution.

P W I N O     5.21 Utilize staff development and training to prepare current employees to accept new or added responsibilities.

P W I N O     5.22 Offer early retirement packages for faculty, administrators, and classified staff only if you hire back at a lower rate of pay than those leaving.

P W I N O     5.23 Postpone solar energy efforts, thus avoiding start-up costs that have a slow payback.

P W I N O     5.24 Defer replacement of aging equipment, frayed drapes, worn carpets, and so forth.

## Reduced Services across-the-Board

P W I N O    5.25 Arrange for all staff members (administrative, classified, support, etc.) to take one unpaid day of leave per month as agreed with their immediate supervisor.

P W I N O    5.26 Reduce the contracts for administrators, instructors, and classified staff by ten working days per fiscal year.

P W I N O    5.27 Require that the summer months of all twelve-month appointments be "self-supporting."

P W I N O    5.28 Consider a four-day class schedule and workweek during the academic year.

P W I N O    5.29 Close the campus for one or two weeks between summer session and fall term, and furlough staff.

## Elimination or Dramatic Reduction
## of Programs or Administrative Functions

P W I N O    5.30 Streamline the organization by eliminating one or more deanships.

P W I N O    5.31 Eliminate full-time faculty positions in areas of low enrollment, such as foreign languages or music.

P W I N O    5.32 Implement a reduction-in-force plan derived through a zero-based budgeting process.

P W I N O    5.33 Freeze or restrict the hiring of part-time instructional staff, thus reducing course offerings in developmental education, adult self-improvement, and other areas.

P W I N O    5.34 Limit summer school facilities and offerings to one campus.

P W I N O    5.35 Eliminate the summer session entirely.

## Curriculum and Instruction

*Curriculum*

P W I N O    5.36 Provide ongoing review of course offerings to determine their viability for programs, community needs, course needs, course enrollments, comparative cost effectiveness, budgetary considerations, and so forth.

P W I N O  5.37 Offer some transfer courses on an alternate year basis.

P W I N O  5.38 Increase average class size: (1) offer some classes less often during the year, (2) cancel small classes quickly and advise students into other classes, and/or (3) change program requirements with fewer choices to students.

P W I N O  5.39 Give instructors the option to teach fewer students for less pay, down to a predetermined minimum.

P W I N O  5.40 Shorten fall and winter terms to eight weeks, and spring term to six weeks.

P W I N O  5.41 Contract with local school districts to operate programs with low enrollments.

P W I N O  5.42 Share instructors with nearby college districts through teleconferencing. Low enrollment classes and programs can be filled at one-half the cost of instruction.

P W I N O  5.43 Eliminate instructional programs in small communities unless the number of tuition-paying students provides for full cost of offerings.

P W I N O  5.44 "Double-list" course offerings in small communities (credit/noncredit).

P W I N O  5.45 Secure a volunteer community coordinator to plan schedules in small rural towns; provide the volunteer with free classes in return.

P W I N O  5.46 Close a center if an alternative nearby can provide the same service.

P W I N O  5.47 Secure charitable agency funding to offset the cost of classes of direct interest or benefit—for example, March of Dimes for childbirth preparation, teen parenting, prenatal care.

P W I N O  5.48 Contract for services with businesses and agencies to reduce costs and dependence on FTE. Offer courses, seminars, and workshops on a cost-plus basis.

## Instruction

P W I N O        5.49 Develop differentiated staffing for resource centers, such as a differentiated math resource center.

P W I N O        5.50 Assign administrators to duties in instruction or instructional support.

P W I N O        5.51 Investigate classes offered, particularly laboratory classes, to see if all levels could be taught in the same class.

P W I N O        5.52 Carpool all field trips instead of using college vans, passing on the cost to the students.

P W I N O        5.53 Utilize students to grade their own work and record the grades.

P W I N O        5.54 Use advanced students for peer tutoring.

P W I N O        5.55 Utilize volunteer tutors. Expand the tutor coordinator's role to include recruiting and training volunteer tutors for specific assignments.

P W I N O        5.56 Contact local service clubs and seek sponsorship of classes in ESL (English as a second language), adult basic education, and so forth.

## Media

P W I N O        5.57 Telecourses can be used to provide instruction to students in the outreach areas and will allow for additional flexibility on campus. Courses can be offered via cable, PBS, satellite, or V-Tel. Local school districts could use telecourses to augment district staff—for example, science and computer courses.

P W I N O        5.58 Organize a community college consortium for audiovisual software. This group would coordinate the purchasing, renting, and loaning of audiovisual software among community colleges.

P W I N O        5.59 Utilize computers for test review, test generation, and record keeping for telecourses.

P W I N O    5.60 Increase or initiate use of computers for instruction in developmental education, as well as record keeping.

P W I N O    5.61 Freeze spending for equipment, library books, materials, supplies, and outside services.

P W I N O    5.62 Change video format, if you have not already done so, from 3/4-inch and 16mm to 1/2-inch. The 1/2-inch format is approximately 30 percent less expensive than 3/4-inch, and approximately 75 percent less expensive than 16mm.

P W I N O    5.63 Reduce the number of telephones on each campus.


## Student Services

P W I N O    5.64 Instead of mailing grades to students, have students who are in school the next term stop by admissions to pick up grade sheets.

P W I N O    5.65 Eliminate tuition waivers for student body officers and immediate family members of staff.

P W I N O    5.66 Operate selected sports and activities on a club basis, funded by user fees or private organization sponsorship, thus removing them from the general fund budget.

P W I N O    5.67 Eliminate athletic competition in golf, tennis, cross-country, and similar sports. Fund the remaining program with vending machine revenue as supported by student government.

P W I N O    5.68 Eliminate talent grants.

P W I N O    5.69 Discontinue student services as a separate program, requiring that the faculty accept more responsibility in guidance and counseling.

P W I N O    5.70 Assign counselors to teach classes in career planning, job search, test anxiety, study skills techniques, and so on. This could result in less one-on-one counseling.

P W I N O    5.71 Use students to help in replacing or supplementing classified positions.

P W I N O    5.72 Ask every student to donate some work time to the college, even if it is only a few hours per term for part-time students.

P W I N O    5.73 Allow students to barter for waived tuition.

P W I N O    5.74 Consolidate use of Career Information System in a cooperative effort by ESDs, public high schools, and community colleges.

P W I N O    5.75 Implement a yearlong computer produced schedule.

P W I N O    5.76 Revise office procedures so that all registration material is put in to the central computer by the field offices.

P W I N O    5.77 Computerize the student services area, including (1) online registration with associated list generation, (2) financial aid and veterans, (3) follow-up, (4) self-help advising/scheduling/career analysis.

P W I N O    5.78 Review other college publications through sharing arrangements concerned with registration to determine whether their formats are less costly to produce and mail.

P W I N O    5.79 Replace the annually printed and bound adviser's handbook with a three-ring binder into which a loose-leaf handbook, and other documents related to academic advising are placed. Replace annually only those portions that need revision.

## Expanded Cost-saving Ideas

P W I N O    5.80 *Expanded Idea #1.* Increase accident prevention efforts, especially in high-risk areas, focusing on job safety and safety training materials.

P W I N O    5.81 *Expanded Idea #2.* Reduce the contracts for administrators, instructors, and classified staff by ten working days per fiscal year.

P W I N O    5.82 *Expanded Idea #3.* Allow students to barter for waived tuition.

P W I N O   5.84 *Expanded Idea #4.* Replace the annually printed and
bound adviser's handbook with a three-ring binder into
which a loose-leaf handbook, and other documents related
to academic advising are placed.

## CHAPTER 6: GENERATING
## ALTERNATIVE REVENUE SOURCES IN EDUCATION

P W I N O   6.1 "The hottest fund-raising trend in public education is
local education foundations (LEFs). LEFs employ many
fund-raising techniques such as direct solicitation letter
campaigns, use of special credit cards, dinners, golf tournaments, car raffles, and auctions" (De Luna 1998).

P W I N O   6.2 LEFs are nonprofit, tax-exempt third parties that foster
educational innovation and school improvement and help
fill the gap while supplying schools and districts with
needed funds, equipment, and services donated by generous alumni, community members, and businesses who are
able to take a tax deduction.

P W I N O   6.3 LEFs usually provide minigrants to staff and scholarships to students; fund curriculum enrichment programs;
and often underwrite special teaching positions.

P W I N O   6.4 Investigate other creative fund-raising strategies: partnerships with booster clubs and businesses; programs for
soliciting volunteers or businesses for in-kind donations
utilizing tax deductible receipts; selling and leasing services and facilities; generating income from student run
businesses; generating investment income; collecting pay
to play fees to fund sports and cocurricular activities; holding and sponsoring schoolwide fund-raising events such as
bottle and can drives; cooperating with social services
providers through bill back programs to Medicaid; partnerships or interagency agreements with park and recreation
districts to fund certain programs allowing the school dis-

trict to free up funds currently being used on these activities to be used for other high priority school programs and services, and pursuing government and private foundation grants.

P W I N O  6.5 Other fund-raising strategies have included ideas like the following: becoming the area's Internet service provider, renting out buses and drivers to community groups and forest fire fighters, organizing for-profit fish farms and agricultural farm run by students, and school retail stores such as a hardware and farm feed and seed run out of the vocational department who gets materials and supplies at wholesale and sells them at retail.

P W I N O  6.6 More controversial fund-raisers used in some districts include agreements with businesses for allowing advertising on school property, in such areas as:
- Privatization of school programs and services
- Electronic marketing
- Corporate-sponsored educational materials
- Sponsorship of programs and activities
- Exclusive agreements with corporations
- Incentive programs
- Appropriation of space
- Corporate matching programs
- Grocery script and soup label campaigns
- Discount rebates back to schools for referring shoppers to a store

P W I N O  6.7 States have also generated new revenue sources not dependent solely on property taxes, such as funds for schools from state-run lotteries and funds from lawsuit settlements with top tobacco companies.

P W I N O  6.8 Focus the district on the mission of continually improving student learning, achievement, and excellence.

P W I N O  6.9 Lobby local legislators to draft new legislation to increase school funding without increasing property taxes.

P W I N O     6.10 Establish an education foundation.

P W I N O     6.11 Implement a four-day week class schedule.

P W I N O     6.12 Conduct a cost-reduction study and implement the good ideas generated.

P W I N O     6.13 Write grants.

P W I N O     6.14 Expand the district's student population (which works well in states that have formulas for funding basic school support).

P W I N O     6.15 Restructure schooling to expand the curriculum without expanding the staff by implementing distance learning and computer instruction technologies.

P W I N O     6.16 Establish school-business partnerships that raise revenues or increase resources and that are mutually beneficial to the district and the business partner.

P W I N O     6.17 Share costs and services with various districts and agencies, including parks and recreation districts, through consortiums and developing interagency agreements to provide personnel and services at the school site in exchange for use of school facilities when not in use by school students or personnel.

P W I N O     6.18 Plan, develop, and implement various entrepreneurial enterprises and student-run businesses that help to pay for some or all of the class and student run business.

P W I N O     6.19 Stay in a continuous process of school improvement, strategic planning, and change focused on your mission and on increasing revenues and reducing costs.

P W I N O     6.20 Mission: total commitment to excellence through increased efficiency, accountability, service, employee training, increased parent involvement, and service to gain higher student achievement and mastery of the new basics for the twenty-first century.

P W I N O     6.21 Lobby legislators at both the state and federal levels for new funds. Encourage federal legislators to get bills changed at the federal level so these funds can be used in addition to state school support. Continue lobbying legislators with regard to many forms of legislation that will either increase revenue or assist in cutting expenses in our schools.

P W I N O    6.22 Establish an educational foundation that will allow people and businesses to donate money, goods, or services and receive tax write-offs for doing so.

P W I N O    6.23 Conduct a study and implement agreed upon recommendations for cost savings that are feasible.

P W I N O    6.24 Write grants to attract alternative revenue sources. Such grants can either be written by the district, the foundation or both.

P W I N O    6.25 Utilize all appropriate forms of technology to deliver instruction in different ways. Restructure schooling and the delivery of instructional services. Not only maintain current accreditation status with the state but also become a model 21st Century School Site that receives local, state, national, and international recognition.

P W I N O    6.26 Establish school-business partnerships and entrepreneurial enterprises both on and off the school site that generate income and job sites for students in grades 7–12. Use some of the profit generated by these programs to help fund the operational expenses of the program.

P W I N O    6.27 Share costs and services with local area districts, the ESD, a consortium of districts, county and state agencies, the business sector, and higher education while still maintaining the school's identity and autonomy.

P W I N O    6.28 Conduct further study and gain public input on the concept of voting to develop a small parks and recreation district for the full funding of such high school programs as arts, crafts, and woodshop, music, outdoor education, interscholastic athletics, performing arts, vocational agriculture, and home economics.

P W I N O     6.29 Continue to add other ideas for generating alternative revenues not solely dependent on property taxes. Implement these new ideas as the board, staff, administration, parents, students, and public are able to reach consensus on them. Brainstorm now to generate more quality ideas.

# Appendix C

## Submit Your Own Creative Ideas
## for Cutting Costs and Generating Revenues

To: Tim Adsit, POB 861, Crane, Oregon 97732

*Directions:* If you have an idea or if you have tried an idea that has resulted in either greater efficiency/productivity, cut costs, or generated revenues not dependent solely on property taxes, please share it with us. Please describe the idea and include any supportive comments or documentation in the space provided or on the back of this form. Each idea should be analyzed according to the following format:

1. Description of the idea: (Circle One) Cost-savings or Revenue Generating. Please describe:


2. Legal or illegal at the present time in this state? (Circle One) Legal or Illegal.


3. Estimated savings or revenue from implementing the idea: (Explain)

4. Estimated time to implement the idea: (Explain)


5. Priority of implementing the idea: (Circle One)
   Extremely Crucial      Crucial  Important      Not Important at the
                                                  Present Time


6. Who is responsible for the idea's implementation? (Write Name or Description)


7. Recommendations, if any:


8. Estimated impact, cost savings, or revenues to be generated from implementing the idea:


9. Idea submitted by:
   Name:_____
   Address:_____
   City:_____
   State:_____
   Zip:_____
   Telephone:_____

# References

Adsit, T. L. 1995. Are there effective school funding alternatives beyond property taxes? Speech and written presentation in booklet form given at the National School Boards Association, fifty-fifth annual conference and exposition, San Francisco, Calif., April 2.

Berliner, D. 1983. The executive functions of teaching. *Instructor* 93, no. 2 (September): 28–40.

Blake, R. R., and J. S. Mouton. 1964. *The managerial grid*. Houston, Tex.: Gulf Publishing.

Bourgeois, L. J. 1985. Strategic goals, perceived uncertainty and economic performance in volatile environments. *Academy of Management Journal* 28:548–73.

Brophy, J. 1979. Teacher behavior and its effects. *Journal of Educational Psychology* 71, no. 6:733–50.

Brown, O. 1978. Pages and pages on how to cut school costs in your school system. *American School Board Journal* (October): 32–45.

Business Task Force on Education, Associated Oregon Industries. 1969. Public School Survey and Recommendations.

De Luna, P. 1998. Local education foundations: Right for many schools. *Phi Delta Kappan* 79, no. 5 (January): 385–89.

Dodds, D. R. 1990. Managing decline: A study to identify the leadership strategies and skills used by Oregon public school superintendents to manage organizational decline. PhD dissertation, University of Oregon.

Doherty, V., and J. Fenwick. 1982. Can budget reduction be rational? *Educational Leadership* 39, no. 4 (January): 252–57.

Dunnette, M. D. 1964. Predictors of executive effectiveness. In *Measuring Executive Effectiveness*, ed. F. R. Wickert and D. E. McFarland. New York: Appleton-Century Crofts.

Einstein, Albert. http://en.thinkexist.com/quotation/problems_cannot_be_solved_by_the_same_level_of/222020.html.

French, J. P., Jr., and B. Ravin. 1985. The social bases of power. In *Studies in social power*, ed. D. Cartwright, 150–67. Ann Arbor: University of Michigan Press.

Gallop Organization and Phi Delta Kappa Poll. 2002. Americans list biggest challenges of U.S. schools, December 3, available from www.gallup.com/poll/tb/educYouth/.

————. 2001. Gallop/Phi Delta Kappa Poll on Education.

Garrett, T. A. Earmarked lottery revenues for education: a new test of fungibility. *Journal of Education Finance* 26, no. 3 (Winter 2001): 219–38.

Governmental Accounting Standards Board, Statement 34. Governmental Accounting Standards Board, available at: asbointl.org\Publications\Publications Online\index.asp?bid=942.

Hadderman, M. 1998. *School productivity*. ERIC Digest. Eugene, OR: ERIC Clearinghouse on Educational Management.

Hanushek, E. A. 1996. School resources and student performance. In *Does money matter?* ed. Gary Burtless, 43–73. Washington, D.C.: Brookings Institution Press.

Hardy, C. 1987. Investing in retrenchment: Avoiding the hidden cost. *California Management Review* 29, no. 4.

Hawley, W., and S. Rosenholtz, with H. Goodstein and T. Hasselbring. 1984. Good schools: What research says about improving student achievement. *Peabody Journal of Education* 61, no. 4 (Summer).

Hedges, L. V., R. D. Laine, and R. Greenwald. 1994. Does money matter? A meta-analysis of studies of the effects of differential school inputs on student outcomes. *Educational Researcher* 23, no. 3 (April): 5–14.

Hefty, J. C. 1981. *A handbook for coping with decelerating resources*. Denver: University of Denver and Colorado Department of Education.

Heiligman, N. 2002. PowerPoint presentation to the Oregon State Legislature, May and September.

Herman, C. F. 1972. Threat, time and surprise: A simulation of international crisis. In *International crisis: Insights from behavioral research*, ed. C. F. Herman, 187–211. New York: Free Press.

Johnston, R. C. 1998. Study documents shifts in district's spending. *Education Week* 18, no. 9 (January 14).

Kazal-Thresher, D. M. 1993. Educational expenditures and school achievement: When and how money can make a difference. *Educational Researcher* 22, no. 2 (March): 30–32.

Levine, C. H. 1978. Organizational decline and cutback management. *Public Administration Review* 38:316–25.

———. 1985. From decrementalism to strategic thinking: Police management in the 1980s. *Public Administration Review* 25:691–99.

Littlejohn, R. F. 1983. *Crisis management: A team approach*. New York: American Management.

Managing costs creatively—MC2 project. 1982. Oregon Department of Education (Spring).

Manzo, K. K. 2000. Study offers new insights on state lotteries. *Education Week* (November 1): 21.

McKelvey, B. 1988. Organizational decline from a population perspective. In *Readings in Organizational Decline*, ed. K. S. Cameron, R. I. Sutton, and D. A. Whetten, 399–410. Cambridge, Mass.: Ballinger.

Merz, C., and S. S. Frankel. 1997. School foundations: Local control or equity circumvented? *School Administrator* 54, no. 1 (January): 28–31.

Miles, R. E., and C. C. Snow. 1978. *Organizational strategy, structure and process*. New York: McGraw-Hill.

Miller, B. A. 1991. *Distress and survival: Rural schools, education and the importance of community*. Portland, Ore.: Northwest Regional Educational Laboratory Rural Education Program.

Miller, K. & I. Iscoe. 1963. The concept of crisis. *Human Organization* 22 (Fall): 195–201.

Molnar, A., and J. Morales. 2000. Commercialism @ Schools. *Education Leadership* 58, no. 2 (October): 39–44.

Monk, D. H., and B. O. Brent. 1997. *Raising money for education: A guide to the property tax*. Thousand Oaks, Calif.: Corwin Press.

Monk, D. H., and E. J. Haller. 1986. *Organizational alternatives for small rural schools: Final report to the legislature of the state of New York*. New York: Cornell University.

National Center for Education Statistics. 1999. Washington, D.C.: U.S. Department of Education, from projections website http://nces.ed.gov/.

———. 2000. Estimated revenues and expenditures for public elementary and secondary education: School year 2000–01. Washington, D.C.: U.S. Department of Education.

National Conference of State Legislatures. 1996. The search for equity in school funding. Education Partners Project Working Paper, Denver, Colo.

News Bytes. 2001. *Confederation of Oregon School Administrators* 1, no. 1 (June).

*Northwest Energy Management Handbook* (March 1980).

Odden, A., and W. Clune. 1995. Improving educational productivity and school finance. *Educational Researcher* 24, no. 9 (December): 6–10.

Oregon Legislative Revenue Office. 2002. *The economic and revenue forecast document, Oregon Department of Administrative Services, September 2001, Economic Forecast.*

Parrish, T. B. 2000. Special education costs. *School Business Affairs* 66, no. 8 (August): 39–43.

Pijanowski, J. C., and D. H. Monk. 1996. Alternative school revenue sources: There are many fish in the sea. *School Business Affairs* 62, no. 7 (July): 4–6, 8–10.

Protheroe, N. 1997. ERS—Local school budget profile study. *School Business Affairs* 63, no. 10 (October): 42–49.

Smart, C. A. 1980. A study of executive perceptions of corporate crisis. PhD dissertation, University of British Columbia.

Stallings, J. 1980. Allocated academic learning time revisited, or beyond time on task. *Educational Researcher* 9, no. 11:11–16.

Sutton, I. 1983. Managing organizational death. *Human Resource Management* 22:391–412.

*The Oregonian.* 2001. September 2.

Thomas, K. W. 1976. Conflict and conflict management. In *Handbook of Industrial and Organizational Psychology*, ed. M. D. Dunnette. Chicago: Rand McNally.

U.S. Department of Education. 1997. *Profile of the Department of Education.* Annual Accountability Report: Fiscal Year 1996. Washington, D.C.: U.S. Department of Education, 1997.

Walberg, H. J. 1984. What makes schools effective? A synthesis and a critique of three national studies. *Contemporary Education: Journal of Reviews* 1, no. 1:22–34.

Whetten, D. A. 1980. Organizational decline: A neglected topic in organizational science. *Academy of Management Review* 5, no. 4:577–88.

Wiener, A. J., and H. Kahn. 1962. *Crisis and arms control.* Harmon-on-Hudson Institute.

Zammuto, R. F., and K. S. Cameron. 1982. Environmental decline and organizational response. In *Proceedings of the Academy of Management Annual Meeting*, ed. K. H. Chung, 250–55. New York: Academy of Management.

# Index

# About the Authors

**Tim Adsit** has served as a professional executive administrator throughout his career in school districts that value visionary leadership and continuous improvement in student learning and achievement.

Since 2001, Tim has been serving as superintendent/principal of Harney County School Districts # 1J and 4 located in Crane, Oregon. Prior to taking over in Crane, Adsit spent four years as director of curriculum and grant-writing in Brookings-Harbor School District, Brookings, Oregon, and six years as superintendent/principal in Perrydale School District, Perrydale, Oregon. He has served as a director of personnel and assessment, rural school supervisor, director of special education, management consultant, elementary and secondary principal, and middle school teacher. He has also consulted with numerous school districts across the United States on "Strategic Planning" and "Generating Effective School Funding Alternatives Beyond Dependence on Property Taxes."

He received his MEd and BS in education from Oregan State University, and did post-graduate work in educational administration at the University of Oregon.

**George Murdock** has been serving as superintendent of the Umatilla-Morrow Education Service District since 1999. During the 2003–2004 school year, he also served as superintendent of the Ione School District and headed the Morrow County School District.

Prior to taking over the ESD in Pendleton, Murdock spent six years as superintendent of the Pasco School District and eleven years as deputy superintendent of the Walla Walla School District. He has also been a high school principal, a high school assistant principal, and a classroom teacher. In 1997, he was named Washington's Superintendent of the Year.

He received his MEd from Linfield College, McMinnville, Oregon, and his BS in agriculture and journalism from Washington State University.

Murdock in the executive director of the Oregon Small Schools Association and is serving a two-year term as president of the Oregon Association of Education Service Districts.